Won't Back Down

Won't
Back Down

Teams, Dreams, and Family

KIM MULKEY

with **Peter May**

Foreword by Pat Summitt

Da Capo Press
A Member of the Perseus Books Group

Set in Cheltenham

Cataloging-in-Publication data for this book is available from the Library of Congress.

First Da Capo Press edition 2007
First Da Capo Press paperback edition 2008
ISBN-10 0-306-81746-2
ISBN-13 978-0-306-81746-5

Published by Da Capo Press
A Member of the Perseus Books Group
www.dacapopress.com

Da Capo Press books are available at special discounts for bulk purchases in the U.S. by corporations, institutions, and other organizations. For more information, please contact the Special Markets Department at the Perseus Books Group, 2300 Chestnut Street, Suite 200, Philadelphia, PA 19103, or call (800) 810-4145, ext. 5000,or e-mail special.markets@perseusbooks.com.

To Makenzie and Kramer—the loves of my life.
It is my hope that I have taught you, by example,
the meaning of dedication, commitment, and loyalty.
Allow those qualities to permeate your lives and to
forever be a measurement of who you are.
Above all, stand your ground—and don't back down.

Contents

Foreword

by Pat Summit

For the longest time, I have had great respect for Kim Mulkey. When she played against Tennessee as a point guard at Louisiana Tech, she always had such a fiery personality and competitiveness about her. I admired her toughness and the way she ran that team. She was such a student of the game.

That Louisiana Tech program was one that helped me a lot as I started to build the Tennessee program. You have to figure out how you are going to play against and eventually beat the best. They were the best back then, in the early 1980s, and Kim was a big part of their success.

In thinking back to the times I coached against her and the times that I coached her on the 1984 Olympic team, I can't recall a single instance where she wasn't totally focused on the game. She was determined to be the best she could possibly be, whether that came in the form of running the Louisiana Tech basketball team or coaching the Baylor team. She puts her heart and soul into everything she does.

What Kim accomplished at Baylor is remarkable. Before she got there, no one thought of Baylor as a Final Four or a National Championship team. Nevertheless, she did it, she did it the right way—bringing out the absolute best in the players she had—and she did it in record time. You saw the personality of that team through its head coach. I went to seven Final Fours before I finally cut the nets down. She did it in her first. How many coaches enjoy that kind of instant success?

I look at Kim today and I see a great role model for the young women of today. She is passionate. She is caring. She has found a balance in her life between her job and raising her two children. She is bright and articulate, and she can teach and motivate young people.

Mostly when I think of Kim, though, I think of the player or the coach who has an insatiable drive and will to succeed. That has allowed her to have the success she has had, as both a player and a coach. No woman had ever won an NCAA championship as a player, assistant coach, and head coach until Kim did it in 2005.

I think Kim would have been a success in whatever field she chose. That she chose women's college basketball only makes the game better. Those that get a chance to play for her will be better equipped to handle the real world when they leave Baylor, with the degree they earned in the classroom and the life lessons they learned on the basketball court.

Prologue

❦

April 5, 2005
NCAA Championship Game
Baylor University vs. Michigan State University
Time Remaining: 2 minutes, 49 seconds
Score: Baylor 78, Michigan State 58

❦

That's when it really hit me; we were going to win a National Championship. I looked up at the clock and we had a 20-point lead and I remember saying to myself, "Coach, you can't possibly screw this up. If you have to milk it, milk it. But you cannot screw this up." I turned around and looked at my assistants, who had been with me through all of it. I looked at my bench. Then I did something I never do: I looked over at the Baylor fans in the stands across the court, my eyes traveling from the bottom seats to the top seats. And for the first time, I realized how many of our fans were there. They were everywhere. I told myself, "Take this in. You're getting ready to win a National Championship."

☾☾

Time Remaining: 30 seconds
Score: Baylor 84–62

☾☾

The only thing I can remember at the end is grabbing my assistants and hugging them. I can still see my kids, Makenzie and Kramer, in a dead sprint running across the floor to hug their mother. There's no greater feeling in the world than to have your children and husband sharing in anything good that happens in your career because they certainly get the brunt of anything that's bad when you go home or when you're at a loss for words after a defeat. I needed to brace myself. I was thinking, "Don't run too fast kids, I'm wearing heels and you'll knock mama over." I was squeezing my nose with my finger and squinting, trying not to cry. Everything was happening so fast. The players were scattering everywhere. I was trying to acknowledge my family and my friends in the stands. There was confetti and streamers flying and fireworks going off. It seemed surreal. It's a memory I will never forget and it's a feeling that will never ever go away.

After the game we received a police escort back to the hotel. We went into a large ballroom where the WBCA (Women's Basketball Coaches Association) presented us with the Avis WBCA championship trophy. It seemed like there were thousands of people there. We signed autographs after the presentation for about an hour and then I went back to my room. Friends and family visited with me into the wee hours of the night. I then got into my sleep shirt, sat in my bed under the covers, and began answering all the emails, text messages, and phone messages from former players, friends, and coaches. I was not ready to go to sleep quite yet.

I woke up the next morning and did an interview on ESPN's television show, *Cold Pizza*. I did more interviews and then I received a phone call from President Bush, who was on Air Force One on the way to the Pope's funeral. We talked for about five minutes. It was a pretty generic conversation with him offering his congratulations, but it was still a phone call from the President of United States of America!

I hung up the phone after talking with the the president and I remember thinking once again: We won a national championship! You're just not supposed to win a championship in five years. There's no formula to follow for winning a championship that quickly. There's no precedent.

When I look back on that year and on all the things that happened in my life that led to that moment, I think of that song by Tom Petty, "Won't Back Down." There are some lines that speak to everything I'd done, such as "Well I know what's right, I got just one life, in a world that keeps on pushing me around but I'll stand my ground. And I won't back down."

Those words not only tell the story of my life, but they also tell the story of that magical season. We didn't back down. We stood our ground—and we prevailed in the end. How did it happen? Well, a lot of things had to take place in my life to get me to that special moment.

The Hammond Honey

I was born at St. Joseph's Hospital in Santa Ana, California on May 17, 1962. My given name was supposed to be Kimberly Duan Mulkey. Duan is not a family name, but my mother liked it and wanted it for my middle name. Somehow, however, the name on the birth certificate ended up "Duane," so my legal name is actually Kimberly Duane Mulkey. People always ask where the name Duane came from, and well, that's the story. It probably would have caused just as much curiosity if my name was Duan.

I only know a few details about my parents' younger days. My father picked strawberries and milked cows when he was a kid in Hammond, Louisiana. My mother grew up in Alexandria, Louisiana, but her family moved to Hammond when she was in high school. My parents met at a swimming pool in town.

Both of my parents were fairly athletic. I think you could best describe my dad as a recreational athlete. During his school years, he played football and basketball at Hammond High. After high school, he attended college at Southeastern Louisiana University for a while but left college to enlist in the Marine Corps. My mother played basketball for Hammond High but didn't play beyond the high school level. After she graduated, she went to Baton Rouge for a year to attend beautician school and married my father shortly after finishing. Dad still had 15 months left in the Marine Corps when they married, so after the ceremony, they moved back to California where he was in the Air Wing unit stationed at the base in El Toro.

When I was still a baby my father's military commitment ended and he moved our family back to Hammond where his family owned land. We settled back in Louisiana and my father worked in the pest control business while my mother operated a beauty shop out of our house.

Technically, our house was located in Tickfaw, which is north of Hammond, but I always attended the Hammond schools. Natalbany, which is another small town between Hammond and Tickfaw, was where our family attended church. All three communities, at one time or another, have claimed to be my hometown. So in the interest of being fair, I just say that I consider myself from Tangipahoa Parish, which is the parish for all three communities.

The home where I grew up was wonderful. It was a one-story, brick, ranch-style house located well off the main road known as Cherry Street Extension. We had a white picket fence in the front yard and a swimming pool in the backyard. My father built my younger sister, Tammy, and me a small basketball court and I spent countless hours there. The warm childhood memories of shooting and dribbling the basketball on that court are what led me later to build one for my own children.

When you drive by the property on Cherry Street Extension today you can't even see the house from the road because of the trees and bushes that have grown since we left. Nevertheless, when I lived there all you could see were big open fields, everywhere. It was a beautiful place to grow up.

It was there that my self-employed parents worked hard to make a comfortable, middle-income home for Tammy and me. They avoided spoiling us but made certain we had nice things. I remember it being very important to my mother that we were well-dressed so twice a year we made the 30-minute drive to Godchaux's clothing store in Baton Rouge for new clothes. She wanted us to be the best-dressed little girls in Hammond, dressing us in neat, clean outfits. My mother allowed us to be ourselves and to do what we enjoyed doing, whether it was playing basketball or riding horses. She was never pushy, just supportive. Without a doubt, both of my parents were very proud of my sister and me. We could always count on them to be there cheering for us at every event in which we participated.

Because we lived in the country I didn't have the experience of growing up in a neighborhood. I spent the majority of my time around family. Our neighbors were my grandparents, who lived across the pasture, and my aunts and uncles, who lived down the road. Instead of socializing and playing with neighborhood kids, I had my cousins and Tammy. It wasn't a chore to spend time with my relatives. I got pleasure out of simple things and loved being around them. My "buddies," as a result, were mostly adults. I was perfectly content to sit with older people talking, eating, watching television, or doing whatever else they might do after a long day of work. Hanging out with the family was my idea of fun. I didn't have a best friend and didn't really need one. While I did have some friends and acquaintances, I don't remember ever spending the night at another girl's home while growing up. My own bed and my own bathtub, in my own home, was what I preferred.

As I grew up, surrounded by the beauty of the Louisiana countryside and the comfort of family, I set values and established high standards for myself. I knew all along what I wanted: I wanted to be the best at whatever I did. Playing sports to the best of my ability made me feel good. My parents didn't heavily emphasize academics, but my schooling was very important to me. Competing in the classroom made me feel good. Whether applying myself physically or academically, I gave everything I could to the challenge before me. To this day, I continue to strive to do my best and to set high standards for myself and for those around me.

In 1968, I started the first grade at Woodland Park Elementary School. Of course, I didn't know anything about *Brown v. the Board of Education,* the 1964 Civil Rights Act, or what would soon be court-ordered integration in southeastern Louisiana. When I was seven years old and starting the second grade I had my first exposure to integration. I returned to school that fall expecting to pick up where I had left off the year before but quickly discovered that wasn't the case. A lot of the white kids were gone and things were completely different. As young as I was, I knew something had changed. A lot of the teachers were the same, but I remember thinking that maybe I was at the wrong school. After school I went home and asked my mother where all of my schoolmates from the year before had gone. She sat me down, and as bluntly but gently as she could, explained what was going on. It really made an impression on me because I remember responding, "People left the school because black people were coming?" I couldn't comprehend it. She explained that changes were taking place and most people didn't like change. All those white students were now at another school. That was all she needed to tell me; we never discussed it again. Even at that age I had a sense of what was right and wrong. My mother predicted that by the time I reached high school all of the kids who had left the public schools would be back and everything would work itself out. She was right. Most of them did return.

Staying in public school played a major role in my life and made me who I am today. I believe it was the best education available to me and I will never forget the impact it had on me. I would sit in the front row of the classroom, trying to be the best student I could be and learning how to respect people from different cultures, religions, and walks of life. My positive feelings for the education I received run so deep that I have contributed money to all the public schools I attended.

Growing up in southeast Louisiana I really knew nothing about the rest of the state. I was a country kid and enjoyed a simple life. We didn't travel much, in fact, I can only remember one family vacation; we drove to the West Coast to visit friends in California. Other than that, we made an occasional drive to visit friends in New Orleans (about 45 minutes away) during Mardi Gras season. After experiencing my first Mardi Gras parade, however, I had absolutely no interest in going again. Nevertheless, I would highly recommend that everyone go at least once to experience and appreciate New Orleans culture.

Southern Louisiana's dominant religion is Roman Catholic. Northern Louisiana, where I went to college, is mostly Baptist and Methodist. Regardless of the denomination, religion plays a big part in most southerners' lives. Religion was not crammed down our throats by my parents. We did, however, attend church and Sunday school most Sundays. During my college years, I attended and eventually joined the Methodist church and I am still a Methodist today.

However, I grew up a Baptist. My grandparents were Baptists and my paternal grandmother was a devout practitioner at the Baptist church we attended in Natalbany. Every family at our church seemed to have its own pew. My grandmother, who I called Maw Maw, sat in the back left pew as you entered the church from the rear. I always sat right next to her. She was a very big woman, weighing more than 200 pounds. She never missed a Sunday and was always the one the church called when a function needed her delicious chicken salad sandwiches. Maw Maw was one of my biggest fans and I loved spending time with her. I spent countless hours during my youth sitting on her front porch eating her biscuits, fried chicken, bacon slabs, and drinking Barq's root beer. Maw Maw's formal name was Dorothy Booth Mulkey. She was a strong woman who always let you know if she felt someone had wronged her or a member of her family. Maw Maw was very proud of her grandchildren and her family. I'm a lot like her in that she was an incredibly observant individual. She also liked to eat just as much as I do. And I never ever saw her drink a drop of alcohol.

When I wasn't with Maw Maw I was shooting baskets in the backyard, swimming, or playing baseball or football in the front yard with a cousin. Almost everyone was older than I was, but they still allowed me to hang out with them. My sister Tammy was one of the few relatives younger than me. We were born 11 months apart but for all our closeness in age, we were so different that there could have been decades between us. Tammy liked animals and the rodeo scene. I, on the other hand, didn't have much interest in animals and spent my time studying and playing ball. We were nothing alike—in the classroom, in how we dressed, or in how we acted. The only thing we had in common were our parents. She would do her thing and I would do mine. But we did play on the Hammond High basketball team together.

When I was younger I did some tap and ballet dancing and even played the piano. The first competition I ever entered, however, was a roller-skating marathon. Every Friday and Saturday night the Nettles Skating Rink was open from 7:00 until 10:00 p.m. and Maw Maw would take me skating. I loved to skate and would glide around from the time they opened until they shooed the last of us out the door at closing time. Skating was a big deal for a lot of people back then. I took it seriously enough that I had my own skates with adjustable wheels and my own case for carrying them.

When I was 12 I signed up for a skating marathon and came in fourth place. It was not age-specific and adults signed up as well. The three people that finished ahead of me were all older. Every two hours we were allowed a 10-minute break to take off our skates, massage our feet, get a drink, eat a sandwich, or run to the bathroom. We didn't have to skate fast; we just had to keep moving, around and around the rink while the music kept playing.

I skated for 23 hours and 55 minutes—only five minutes short of skating for an entire day! The only reason I stopped was because my grandfather walked into the rink to check on me. Without thinking (I was sleep skating, I guess) I skated right up to him and started talking. I was immediately disqualified because once you stopped skating, you were out. As soon as I started talking to him I realized what I had done and said to myself, "Oh my gosh, I've just been disqualified!" I was so mad at myself.

By this time in my life I discovered what I liked to do the most—play sports. It didn't matter what the sport was. It could be marbles or spinning tops. It could be touch football, which I played on Sundays with friends who lived in Natalbany, or it could be baseball. Most of my friends were boys and they would probably tell you that I held my own. Whatever was going on, I was doing it. That's how I got involved with organized baseball.

I started playing Dixie Youth baseball when I was 12. I picked up a form one day at school and brought it home. There were tryouts and I wanted to play. I didn't want to play baseball just to be seen as someone trying to break the gender barrier. I wanted to play baseball because I simply had nothing else to do during the summers. There was no basketball for girls and no softball for girls my age. Baseball was all Hammond offered and I knew I was good enough to be one of the first ones picked. I knew I could play with the boys because I already played with them at school during recess. The boys didn't seem to have a problem with it, nor did I think they would. I went straight from school wearing blue jeans, tennis shoes, a T- shirt, and my red, white, and blue baseball glove in hope of being selected for one of the teams. There were lots of boys there, but I was the only girl. I was the first player picked in the draft and played three years of baseball from the time I was 12 until I turned 14. I was the only girl in the league.

I was the first player picked in the draft which meant that I was drafted by the team that had the worst record the previous season. I believe I was selected first because of my ability as a player not because I was a girl. It felt natural for me to be trying out; I was just playing ball.

When I speak at events today I ask parents not to put their daughters in situations where they're attempting to play with boys if their daughters are not good enough. I encourage them to do it for the right reasons—do it because she is good enough. Above all, you need to respect the game. That's why I did it.

I played shortstop, catcher, and pitcher. In the Pony League, which is for 13- and 14-year-olds, I moved to second base and made the All-Star team my second year. My three years of playing baseball were wonderful except for one incident during my 12-year-old season.

During my first year, our Dixie Youth baseball team played in the Dixie Youth Baseball All-Star Tournament in Ponchatoula. I found out I wouldn't be allowed to play because I was a girl. The baseball officials said it was a bookkeeping issue because I was a late addition to our team's roster as an alternate. However, I learned later that Dixie League officials admitted that I wouldn't have been able to play even if I was on the roster.

I still, to this day, don't know why my team listed me as an alternate because I played in all the games and was told that I was selected for the All-Star team. My father was so mad that he hired a lawyer and we went before a judge to get a temporary restraining order preventing the tournament from continuing unless my name was allowed on the roster. Eventually, it came down to me either trying to play and my team forfeiting the game or me watching the game. It didn't seem fair to me, but that was the choice.

Everything was a blur that day. I just wanted to sit on the bench with my teammates. This led to a lot of arguing among the parents at the game and I was ordered to leave the Hammond dugout. I left but came back a short time later with my father. We were both told to leave and we did. I then tried one more time to sit with my teammates. I was told to leave again.

I was left with a tough choice to make: I could try to play and my team would have to forfeit the game or I could choose not to play. I didn't play. My father called the judge and had the restraining order withdrawn. I didn't want to force the issue and punish the rest of the team. In the end, I stood alongside the fence near the dugout watching the game and crying. I didn't think it was fair but that's the way it was. All I wanted to do was play baseball, but the commissioner wouldn't even let me sit on the bench with my team.

Our team won the game and my teammates dedicated it to me. Afterward, they tipped their hats to me as they walked off the field past where I was standing outside the dugout.

I can remember some 10 years later the local Chamber of Commerce was honoring me and the man who introduced me was a former commissioner of the Dixie Youth baseball league. He apologized to me and told me that I should feel proud because I helped open some doors for other girls to play baseball. That was not my intention, but it is nice to think that what I did may have made the road a little easier for another girl.

I didn't start playing organized basketball until I was in the seventh grade, but by the time I got to high school two years later, I played well enough to make the Hammond High varsity team. We won four state championships in the four years I was there. I never had a real nickname but many people called me "the Pistol Pete of girl's basketball," which was a great compliment because it referenced Pete Maravich, who was an extraordinary player.

I think without question it was my father who got me started playing basketball and all the other sports. He played recreational basketball in the city leagues and I would always tag along to watch his games. At halftime or during timeouts, I would run onto the floor and do some shooting. It was the same thing with softball. I was the daughter who tagged along. There wasn't anyone in our area that I aspired to be like, nor was there anyone in my family. I just loved going to his games and watching him play. When I was home I would shoot for hours at a time in our backyard. Either I would shoot alone and work on things like left-handed lay-ups or free throws or I would play with my father, my sister, or anyone else who came along. My dad and I would have some pretty intense games of one-on-one. Sometimes it would be two-on-one with my sister playing along as well. Tammy suffered from ulcers and sometimes we would be playing and need to stop so she could throw up. Soon enough she would feel better and we would go back to playing. My dad was very competitive and so was I. The older I became the more serious the games got. I remember when I was finally physically able to beat him in a game of one-on-one. As a child, I don't think you ever fully believe that you can beat an adult in a game, but as you grow and mature it does happen.

I never had a coach or person who taught me the basics—not in the conventional sense anyway. I think watching my dad and the other players taught me the game. I also watched a lot of sports on television and tried to remember certain things that I saw so I could implement them into my own play.

Once I began playing on a team my forte became seeing everybody on the floor and getting the ball to the open player quickly. Passing is a forgotten part of the game today. You don't see it anymore because there is so much one-on-one play now. I got a thrill out of throwing a bullet pass through the lane to a teammate for an easy lay-up. I felt a rush of excitement when I did something to get the crowd and my team going. My shot was average at best. I had no rotation on the ball—none whatsoever. But if you left me open, I was going to keep shooting and make enough shots to beat you. If you watched me, however, you weren't beaming, "Whoa, what a beautiful shot that girl has!" I never worked that hard on my shot because I could penetrate past whoever was guarding me and create the shots for my teammates. Despite my lack of an aesthetic shot, I could still score. You can be a scorer and not have a great shot.

My passing and ability to play the game gained the respect of my teammates. My sister recalls, "We just always felt we were going to win because Kim was on our side. Nothing scared her. She was our team leader. She was so focused and determined in getting what she wanted. Other girls our age would go out partying and drinking and have a life. She didn't. You usually would have to come to our house and play ball if you wanted to see Kim."

During my high school years, I played for two coaches. Mary Jo Castell was my coach during my freshman and sophomore years and Iwana McGee was my coach during my junior and senior years. The highlight of my high school playing days was winning four state championships. There was also one particular game that still stands out in my mind; I scored 60 points! I would never do that again in all my years of playing.

One tenuous recollection from my high school career was when an opposing player's mom came down out of the stands and confronted me. She had seen her daughter and me going at it during the game, talking a little smack at each other. The game was tough and the crowd had really been into it. When we won, she just lost control. Nothing ultimately happened, and when I think back on it, it's possible the woman didn't even realize what she was doing. But at the time, it was a frightening moment.

Another bad memory was the footwear we were forced to wear my freshman year. We had to wear these ugly, purple high-top, Chuck Taylor canvas tennis shoes. I hated them. It wasn't the color; I just hated high-tops. Nowadays, of course, everyone wears high-tops.

When you consider nowadays all of the high ticket prices for athletic shoes, sportswear, safety equipment, and dietary supplements, among other things, the simplistic way we approached the sport then is almost comical. It's funny to think back on all of the precautions I didn't take—that no one took. I never taped an ankle and I was fortunate to never have a serious injury. My pre-game meal routine amazes me today. Remember, there were no nutritionists, strength and conditioning coaches, or advisors and counselors, so a pre-game meal for me was roast beef, mashed potatoes, and two slices of lemon icebox pie. Undoubtedly, we all played overweight and under protected.

While I excelled on the basketball court, I also took a lot of pride in my work in the classroom. When I graduated from Hammond High I had a 4.0 grade point average. I never earned anything other than straight A's. I was the senior class valedictorian. Make no mistake, though, I worked hard for those grades.

Tammy recalls of my study habits, "She would stay up studying until three or four in the morning and it wasn't so she could make that high B. It was so she could make that A—and she did. She sure didn't spend her time learning how to cook, though. That woman can't even make a hamburger!"

Math and English were by far the subjects I enjoyed the most. Sentence structure was my thing. I could break down a sentence by subject, verb, adverb, adjective— you name it. It was my cup of tea and I loved it. The part of English that I didn't care for was literature. I didn't particularly like Shakespeare. Somehow I knew those plays and stories weren't going to help me in life, but I knew that sentence structure would. I could see its purpose. I liked math because there was only one answer and I was going to find it! It had a finished product and I could see the result, just like in basketball. You win or you lose. I'm not going to say those two subjects came easily to me because I had to work just as hard at them as I did at other subjects. I just appreciated them because of what I felt I got from them.

I was also proud of my attendance record because I never missed a day of school growing up. The irony is that on the day of the awards assembly to honor me for my attendance record, I was late! I was on a recruiting trip and flying back in a private plane. There was a lot of fog in the area and the plane couldn't land on time; I was an hour late for the assembly honoring my punctuality!

My senior year, after I played my last state championship game, I cried both tears of joy and tears of sadness. Joy, because we won another state championship, and sadness, because it was my last high school game. At the end of the year, there was a celebration held at a local restaurant during which my high school jersey was officially retired.

There were a couple of sports writers that I will always remember because they began following my career in high school. One was a sports writer from the *Baton Rouge Advocate* named Joe Planas. He came up to me after my last high school game and gave me a silver dollar. He said, "I want you to always keep this because if you do, you'll never go broke." I still carry that silver dollar in my wallet today. There was also a sports writer from the Ruston area, Buddy Davis, who gave me the nickname "The Hammond Honey."

≪◎

In her four years at Hammond High School Mulkey scored 4,075 points averaging 28.9 points a game. When she left Hammond in 1980, no high school player, man or woman, had ever scored that many points in a career—and she did much of it playing only about three quarters of a 28-minute game.

She was an AAU All-American for four straight years and an academic All-American for those same four years. She was also the Louisiana High School Player of the Year in 1980 and a *Parade* magazine All-American in the same year.

"She had that flair and charisma to her game," said Iwana McGee, her coach at Hammond. "If you were a bad player, she could make you look good. She's the type of kid that you get once in a lifetime and you thank your lucky stars that she was there when you were there."

"She never was a problem. I always had a rule that if you were late for practice, you had to run laps. It was one lap for every minute you were late. You can imagine that Kim was hardly ever late, but one time, we started practice and she wasn't there. I asked if anyone knew where she was and one of the girls said, 'she's outside in her car.' It turned out she had fallen asleep in the car waiting for practice to begin. She came in and she was laughing. She asked me, 'how many laps do I have to do, coach?' And I said, 'look at your watch.' Sure enough, when practice was over, she ran all the laps she had to run. That might have been the only time I ever had to get on her."

"She was so good she could have gone to any college she wanted to go to," McGee said. "And if there was a professional league for women back then, she could have played in that as well."

18

2

That Little Girl
with the Pigtails

In 1973, the president of Louisiana Tech University, F. Jay Taylor, had a decision to make. His school did not have a single intercollegiate sports program for women. One day he received a visit from a few female students. They asked the president if he had ever considered starting a women's basketball program at the university. Taylor had most definitely been thinking along those lines because many of the high schools in the Ruston area had women's basketball programs and some of the women playing intramural basketball at Louisiana Tech were good enough to play at the collegiate level.

Sonja Hogg, a physical education teacher at the school, was given the job of starting a women's basketball program. The program was launched with high hopes, no scholarships, and a budget of $5,000. The first women's basketball game at Louisiana Tech was played on January 7, 1975 and resulted in a home loss to Southeastern Louisiana. "If there were 45 people at that game," Taylor recalls, "that would have been a generous head count."

Hogg was determined to keep the "women" in women's basketball at Louisiana Tech. She mandated that the women's team uniforms have short sleeves and collars and changed the team nickname from the Bulldogs—too unfeminine—to the Lady Techsters. One of Taylor's decisions before he retired in 1987 was to deny a request from the athletic director to remove the words "Lady Techsters" from the sideline floor at the school's assembly center. "If I am going to remove Lady Techsters, then I am going to remove Bulldogs as well. Neither one of those things is going to happen," he said. And they didn't.

In 1977, Taylor hired a Ruston high school coach and former Louisiana Tech player named Leon Barmore to join the coaching staff as a full-time assistant. In a concession to the times, Barmore's title was Coach of Women's Sports. Hogg said, "It was unusual for a man to work for a woman in Louisiana at that time. The trustees would not have gone along with that." Barmore became the de facto head coach while Hogg, who retained the title of head coach, was more of a recruiter. It proved to be an effective combination. Hogg would get the kids to come and Barmore would coach them.

Kim Mulkey first showed up on Hogg's radar screen when Mulkey was only a freshman at Hammond in the 1977 state tournament. "I saw her lead that team to the state championship and I thought it was just wonderful to see a small child doing all those things," Hogg says today. "I came back the next year and there was Hammond High once again. That got my attention. I told Leon that we needed to take a serious look at this kid."

A few years later, Hogg took a phone call from Mulkey's father wondering what she thought about him buying his daughter a Corvette for a high school graduation present. "I told him, if I had a daughter that had just won four straight state championships, was the valedictorian of her class, and was going to college on a scholarship, I couldn't get to a dealer fast enough to buy one," Hogg said. "But I also told him to hold on to the bill of sale because I didn't want to be accused of buying it."

❦

My decision about where to go to college wasn't an easy one. Many colleges solicited me, but the ones I was most interested in were the University of Texas, Mississippi State University, Louisiana State University, Louisiana Tech University, and the University of Georgia. Deep in my heart, however, I knew that I would never leave Louisiana. There was absolutely no sense of wanderlust. The only real question was whether I was going to go to Louisiana State or Louisiana Tech.

I knew nothing about Louisiana Tech except that Terry Bradshaw had played football there. However, after I went on my first recruiting visit there, I knew immediately that Tech was where I wanted to go. The atmosphere at the basketball game was unbelievable. The gym was packed and the fans hardly ever sat down. I told my mother that I felt like I was at a Baptist revival. It was clear to me that this was what I wanted to be a part of for the next four years. In addition, I was used to winning in high school and I didn't want to go to a college that didn't have an established basketball program with high expectations of success.

Sonja Hogg was one of the best recruiters in the game back then and she worked hard at recruiting me, calling me all the time on the telephone. One time my mother told her to wait a minute and called out loud enough for her to hear, "Kim, it's time to get the pigs in the barn. It's a fixin' to rain." We were, of course, joking with Miss Hogg. There were only a few rules to follow in recruiting then and, unlike today, you could make unlimited telephone calls. She wore out our telephone line.

"I was on the phone with that girl more than any other player I recruited, maybe once or twice a day," Hogg says today. "I can't imagine what it would have been like if we had cell phones back then. I would have never hung up. It got so that I would hand the phone over to my husband and he would continue talking to Kim. I got to know the whole family—the grandmothers, the aunts, the uncles. Pretty soon, I felt like I was part of the family."

"The year before Kim came to Tech we recruited a point guard from Georgia who ended up going to Tennessee, as well as a girl from Tennessee named Jennifer White, who also happened to be a point guard. Jennifer ended up coming to Louisiana Tech at the eleventh hour. She committed without ever having seen the school. Even though we won forty games with Jennifer as the point guard that year, I still kept recruiting Kim. Jennifer and Kim were totally different players. I knew Kim felt good in her own skin and was confident of her ability. We just told her that it wouldn't be like it was for her at Hammond, where she was averaging 30-something points a game. And, she was fine with that."

After I made the decision to attend Louisiana Tech it was hard for me to tell my family, most of whom were Louisiana State fans. They asked me, "Why would you go four hours away to Louisiana Tech, which has five returning starters, three of whom are freshmen, and be part of a team that just went to two straight national Final Fours? Why would you do that?" LSU was so much closer to home, an easy drive. Growing up all I heard was LSU, LSU, LSU. I can still sing their fight song. It was the easy decision. I would have played a lot of minutes and my family and friends could have watched me. However, I made the decision to go to Louisiana Tech and my parents never tried to change my mind. They knew I was an independent young woman and they allowed me to make my own decision. The day I signed my letter of intent to play basketball at Tech was a big deal in the Hammond area. I can still vividly remember the excitement, the house brimming with reporters and friends.

In the early '80s, there were certain things expected of a Lady Techster, on and off the floor. When the team left a restaurant, we would each take a toothpick. However, the rule was that we couldn't use it until we returned to the hotel. It just wasn't ladylike to clean your teeth in public. We also weren't allowed to wear flip-flops or warm-ups to class and when we went on road trips we dressed alike in matching blazers and skirts. If you tried to get kids to do this today, they would laugh at you.

After my freshman season at Louisiana Tech, I started wearing my hair in pigtails for the games. It started by accident. During the summer between my freshman and sophomore years, I was playing AAU basketball with Janice Lawrence, one of my college teammates. She started braiding my hair one day. I had mostly worn a ponytail as a freshman, but this felt different and kind of cool. I guess it became a good luck charm because we always won. When I went back to Tech either Janice or a friend of mine would braid my hair for games. I can remember Buddy Davis, the Ruston sports writer, telling me that mothers of little girls in the area wanted to meet me so they could learn how to braid hair like mine. I never realized that the braids identified me to the extent they did until I was out of college. People remembered me more for how I wore my hair than for how well I played!

Before the start of each season at Louisiana Tech the players were required to run a timed mile. The first time I ran it, I didn't finish. Two weeks before I arrived at school, I spent the night in the hospital having my wisdom teeth extracted. The doctors removed the four teeth, and for some unknown reason, a fifth tooth. (My guess is that this means they won't have any trouble identifying me from dental records when I'm dead and gone.) After the procedure and the recovery time, I was totally out of shape. Boy, I was embarrassed that I couldn't even finish the one-mile run! Nevertheless, I knew we'd run the mile again a few weeks later and I made a vow that I would never be in that position again. I ran and ran until I got in better shape. The next time we ran the timed mile I finished in second place.

As a freshman, I experienced the typical feelings of homesickness and second-guessing my college choice. There were a lot of things I wasn't sure of that first year. I wondered if I made the right decision and even considered transferring. There were times when I'd be in the shower, crying, wondering what I should do. I had never been away from home before and everything was new to me. We were winning, which made it a bit easier, and I was doing well in the classroom, which was just as important to me.

I was joining a team that had gone 40–5 the previous year and their point guard, Jennifer White, was returning.

Jennifer was a different kind of player than me, but she was every bit as competitive as I was and she was determined not to lose her starting job. I didn't like not starting, but I also knew that I was a freshman and didn't know the system just yet. I understood the situation and needed to bide my time. I was confident that if I played well and to the best of my ability, Coach Barmore would eventually play me.

My mother and father attended every home game. I know my father was disappointed that I wasn't starting and playing more. He was never really satisfied that I made the right college choice. I don't think he thought all that much of Coach Barmore, either. It didn't bother my mother as much. She just enjoyed the games when she came. She would sometimes sit next to President Taylor and one time, when we were having some trouble with the referees in a game, she turned to Dr. Taylor and said, "You watch the game. I'll do the cussin'." I know Dr. Taylor got a kick out of that.

My father eventually confronted Coach Barmore after a home game in which we defeated Tennessee. He challenged Coach Barmore about why I wasn't playing more. The simple answer: I hadn't played well enough to beat out Jennifer. I know my father was acting like a lot of parents and only wanted what he thought was best for me, but parents tend to focus only on their own child and not on the entire team. What my father said didn't sit well with Coach Barmore, but he never said anything to me until much later. I will say, if I had known about it at the time, my father and I would have had a huge argument. I would have told him that he was wrong and that he needed to let me fight my own battles. However, I also would have told him that I didn't necessarily disagree with him. I felt that I was better than Jennifer, but I also knew that I was the one at practice every day and I was the one that needed to make Coach Barmore play me more.

In the end, Coach Barmore did start to play me more. I started seven games as a freshman, got a lot of playing time, and led the team in assists. Many times I was referred to as "The Sparkplug" because of what I did when I came off the bench. It seemed that whenever I came in we were always able to extend our lead. My style was exciting. I would run, get the ball up the court, and bring a high level of energy and enthusiasm to the game. I got my teammates going. I got the crowd going. And I would top it all off by making a great pass. It was infectious.

Toward the end of the season I had a heart-to-heart with Coach Barmore about my role and my future on the team. Was I going to continue to come off the bench, being "The Sparkplug," or was my role going to be that of a starter? My approach to the conversation was, "Talk to me, Coach. Don't leave me hanging or second-guessing." That day in the stands of Memorial Gym he reassured me of how important I was to the program. We were undefeated—the best team in the country—and even though I wasn't starting, I still was a big part of the team's success. Ultimately, I don't know if I would have ever left Louisiana Tech but there were moments when I thought, "I need to be on that floor playing now or else."

Coach Barmore convinced me of my importance and we finished my freshman season by beating Tennessee in the AIAW finals in Eugene, Oregon. (AIAW stood for Association for Intercollegiate Athletics for Women, which was founded in 1971. In the early 1980s, the NCAA assumed control of collegiate women's basketball and the AIAW eventually disbanded.) I remember jumping into Coach Barmore's arms after the game and saying to him, "You had better be here for three more years because I'm definitely going to be here for three more years." I knew at that moment that I wasn't going anywhere. Ironically, it was after our earlier season defeat of the University of Tennessee that my father had confronted Coach Barmore about my playing time.

The truth of the matter is that we were so good that it didn't matter who played. You could have split us up into two teams and you still would have had two of the top teams in the country. We had so much depth, and looking back, we really had an amazing run.

My game at Louisiana Tech was pretty much the same as it was at Hammond High School except I didn't need to score as much because of all the great talent we had. I focused on what I did well, penetrating and passing. I could get anyone the ball on a dime—anywhere, anyhow. It didn't matter whether it was behind the back, between the legs, no-look, or over the head. I had great peripheral vision. A guard who can penetrate, who has an explosive first step, and who can find the open player is invaluable to a team. At Louisiana Tech, I had two All-American post players in Janice Lawrence and Pam Kelly to dish it off to. If people pressed us, I was able to burn them at the other end. I wasn't going to jump out of the gym and I wasn't going to beat them with my shot, but I could beat them with my quickness and passing. "Kim didn't have much of an outside shot," recalls Jennifer White. "We would tease her in practice about it. She'd miss 10 straight shots and after she finally made one, she'd say, 'someone better get on me.' She could drive to the basket and penetrate better than anyone, though." Coach Barmore would say, "Kim sees nine people on the court when she plays. Not many people can do that."

Louisiana Tech won 54 straight games during my time there, which was a national record that stood for two decades until the University of Connecticut ripped off 70 straight wins from 2001 to 2003. We were ranked first in the country every week of my first two years, losing just one game out of 70—a three-point defeat on the road at Old Dominion. During my first season at Tech, we went 34–0 and 27 of those victories were by 20 or more points. In my second season, the Lady Techsters went 35–1, 26 of the victories were by 20 or more points.

I thought it would be hard to top that first undefeated season, but you soon find out that at Louisiana Tech only two things really matter in Lady Techster basketball— Final Fours and National Championships. Even today when you enter the Thomas Assembly Center, the only team banners you see are for the years we went to the Final Four. There aren't even conference championship banners because there isn't enough room.

I look back on those two years nostalgically. We only lost one game and won two National Championships. I was a part of what, up until then, was probably the greatest women's college basketball team in history. However, I never stepped back to think, "This is pretty good." Instead I always thought, "This is what you're supposed to do. You compete to win. If you're going to play, you're supposed to try to win." My teammate Jennifer White says today, "I have seen every team that has won the National Championship and I still think our Louisiana Tech teams were some of the best, if not the best. We were smart. We were mean. And, above all, we were talented. The other team was the enemy, that's how we approached it. We knew the consequences of losing and it wasn't good."

In the early years of Louisiana Tech basketball all of the players were assigned a host family. My adoptive family, the Tutens, were my family away from home. Even today, Mary Belle Tuten is one of my closest and dearest friends. "I had absolutely no idea who she was or how well she played in high school," Mary Belle recalls. "She was so focused on athletics and academics that she didn't have time for anything else. She wasn't into parties. She preferred to hang around the house and watch games on television. That was who she was then and continues to be to this day."

During the academic year, I would go over to their house to have a home-cooked meal, do my laundry, and play with their daughters. I remember one time when I cut my eye playing touch football on their lawn and we all agreed not to tell Coach Barmore how it happened. He always warned us about doing stuff like that for obvious reasons. The Tutens ended up adding a room onto their house for me and taking me on family vacations with them. I stayed with them during many winter holidays when school was closed but basketball was still in season. (Many times school holidays occur in the middle of the season. Students can go home on break, but athletes have to remain on campus to attend practices and play games.) Sometimes I'd head over to the Tutens after we returned from a road trip, but I always stopped at my dorm room first and unpacked my things. I know this drove Mary Belle crazy; she wanted me to come over just as I was. Apparently, I suffered from a touch of OCD because I always needed to make sure everything was in its rightful place first.

The Tutens were a second family to me and I was a third daughter to them. However, when Louisiana Tech became a member of the NCAA in my second year, it became illegal for athletes to get any special treatment that was not available to all students. Subsequently, the adoptive parent program ended. Nevertheless, the Tutens and I remain close to this day. They are one of the reasons why I know I made the right choice when I decided to attend Louisiana Tech.

Mary Belle was a professor of Human Ecology at Louisiana Tech and I would frequently stop by her office for advice. During my sophomore year, I told her on one visit that I was dropping zoology because I was convinced that I was going to make a B. I was almost in tears, because until that time, I had gone through all those years in the Hammond public schools and one year at Louisiana Tech without ever earning anything less than an A. Mary Belle was aghast at my decision. She gave me all kinds of grief and told me I didn't need to always be perfect, it was all right to get a B every now and then; the sun would still rise in the morning. The truth was I liked the course and the professor was awesome. I just couldn't pull up my grade. After talking with Mary Belle, I took her advice. I returned to the registrar's office and promptly tore up the drop course form. I did end up with a B and I can still remember Coach Barmore joking that it was finally time to celebrate. In the end, staying in the class was the right thing to do. I received a few more B's before I graduated, but my cumulative GPA was 3.82 and I graduated summa cum laude, which was my goal from the beginning.

After my second season at Louisiana Tech the team moved into the Thomas Assembly Center. The new building seated 8,000, which is 3,000 more than Memorial Gym. Sometimes double-headers were scheduled with the men's team. We always played first. Yet after we finished, you could see people leaving the building. All they wanted was to see the Lady Techsters play. Even when Karl Malone was there, the Lady Techsters were still the toast of the town.

For the first time that I can remember, I missed a couple of games during my junior year at Louisiana Tech, once because I got violently sick with a stomach virus and the other because of a badly sprained ankle. We made it to the championship game that year, and at that point, we had only lost one game—the very first game in the Thomas Assembly Center against Southern Cal. We did, however, beat them in the middle of the season during a rematch on a neutral court in California and had won 30 straight games leading up to the championship game.

We were ranked No. 1 and Southern Cal was ranked No. 2. The two teams had developed a pretty good rivalry in those years. Southern Cal had great players like Cheryl Miller, Cynthia Cooper, and the McGee twins, Paula and Pam. I can still remember the time we played them at home and Paula McGee was bringing the ball up the court in a one-on-one situation. I was back alone in transition defense. I was so pumped during the game that I challenged her with a hand motion like "bring it on." The crowd went nuts. Looking back on it I think, "How stupid was I?" She was 6 feet 2 inches tall and I was 5 feet 4 inches tall. She could have rammed the ball down my throat if she wanted. Luckily for me, my teammates got back in time to help before it ever went that far. "That was typical Kim. She was that crazy," Paula McGee says today. "She would tell me to bring it on, girl! Yup, she'd do that."

In the Final Four game against Southern California, we had a double-digit lead at the half. However, we didn't react well in the second half when Southern Cal went to a full-court press. We didn't handle the press as well as we should have and we didn't do a good job of finding Janice Lawrence, our All-American under the basket.

What I remember most about that Southern California game was the ending. We were down by two points in the final 10 seconds and I had just stolen the ball from a Southern California player. Debra Rodman and I were on a two-on-one break, and just as I made a pass to Debra, Cynthia Cooper stepped in front of me. There was contact. The referees called a charging foul on me. Was it a charge? It was a judgment call. I, of course, didn't think so. Cynthia mentioned the play in her book, *She Got Game,* noting that the charging call "was a bit ironic because no one in America took more charges than Kim Mulkey." That was true. I always prided myself in playing tough and trying to take as many charges as I could in each game. Years later I ran into Cynthia at one of the Final Fours. She is now the head coach at Prairie View University in Texas. She asked me if I remembered her. "How could I ever forget you," I replied as we hugged. "I read your book and you know what? It wasn't a charge!" She knew exactly what I was talking about and we both had a good laugh.

After the charging call Southern California got the ball back and we fouled Cheryl. She missed the free throw, giving us one final chance with about six seconds left in the game. The ball came to me, but I was pretty well hounded by the Southern California defense. I got the ball up the court and managed to get off a desperation shot as the buzzer sounded. We lost, 69 to 67.

"To us, Louisiana Tech was our national rival," Paula says. "I can remember beating them in the first game in their new building and it was SRO, fire marshals were turning people away. It was wild. But we felt that their program represented what the old style of women's basketball was all about. It was small-town, it was southern, and it was the Lady Techsters with those uniforms, complete with sleeves and collars. If you played in Ruston the whole town showed up. We felt like we were the team that took women's basketball from the old style to the mainstream. We were the new face of the sport. We were marketable. We were attractive. We were in Los Angeles and we had that certain appeal. Magic Johnson came to our games. Pat Riley came to our games. Michael Warren, the former UCLA guard and current actor on *Hill Street Blues*, came to our games. We got so much publicity."

My final season at Louisiana Tech ended the same way as the one the previous year—with a loss to Southern California. We had another terrific regular season, finishing 27–2. Our only losses, both on the road, were to Old Dominion and Memphis State, which is now named the University of Memphis. We lost both of those games by a total of five points.

We had a pretty easy time getting to the Final Four, which was held at Pauley Pavilion on the campus of UCLA in 1984. We beat Texas Tech, LSU, and the

University of Texas to get there and all three games were blowouts. Nevertheless, Southern Cal would do it to us again. We had beaten them earlier in the season in a home game in Ruston (75–66) but we lost, 62–57, in the semifinals. I will never forget that game because it was the worst game of my college career. I couldn't make a basket. I was 0-for-6 from the field and I had eight turnovers. It was a tough way to go out.

After returning from the Final Four I went to get my driver's license renewed. During the eye examination, I discovered that I was having trouble locating the position of the red dot on the screen. I went straight to an eye doctor. I'm not sure what the medical term for my problem is called, but in layman's terms, I am legally blind in my right eye. It sounds worse than it actually is because I can still see out of my right eye. I just can't pick out the details. I thought at the time that it was kind of humorous. I was playing all this time with only one good eye; I was compensating for something I never even knew I had.

When Coach Barmore heard about my eye situation he joked, "I thought I was the one with vision problems when you missed those two lay-ups in the game against Southern Cal. I thought I was the one seeing things." However, I didn't miss the easy shots because of my eyesight. I should have been able to make them with my eyes closed.

When my college career ended I had gone to four consecutive Final Fours. The Lady Techsters' record over that stretch was 130–6. The six losses were by a combined total of 21 points. We had won two National Championships and were a runner-up the third time. We had winning streaks of 54 games, 30 games, 18 games, and 16 games. For most of that four-year period Louisiana Tech was the top-ranked team in the country. We were never ranked lower than fifth.

There will never be another era like that at Louisiana Tech. The game has become too good. There are so many exceptional programs for recruits to choose from today. There will never be that kind of depth on one team ever again.

I wore number 20 at Louisiana Tech, the same number I wore at Hammond High School. People always ask me why I wore number 20 and the honest answer is that I don't have a clue. I just took it on the day they handed out the uniforms. There was no special significance to it. The university retired my number and today it is hanging in the Thomas Assembly Center along with the seven other retired uniform numbers.

Recently, I received an email from a woman in Richardson, Texas. In it she wrote, "Although we have never met, I feel like I know you. I watched you play basketball in the Louisiana state high school championships. I was there with East Beauregard as a cheerleader, not as a player. I watched you play at Louisiana Tech, and of course, I watched you lead your Lady Bears to a National Championship. I graduated from Tech in '86. I have a 10-year-old daughter that plays with the same intensity that

I saw you play with over the years. That is why I am writing to ask you about your jersey number. I would like for my daughter, Ashley, to wear your number." I answered the email and told the woman that it was number 20. She responded, "I told Ashley it was an honor and she would have to live up to that number by putting in a lot of hard work."

∂⊙

Dr. Taylor recalled being on a trip one time and sitting next to a man on an airplane. When Taylor asked the man where he was going the man replied, "Ruston, Louisiana." He further said he was going there to recruit graduates for his company.

Taylor asked the man how he first heard of the university. "The women's basketball team," the man replied. "And the one player that I will always remember is that little girl with the pigtails."

On the last day of February 1985, nine months after she graduated from Louisiana Tech, Mulkey was honored by the State of Louisiana, receiving the prestigious James J. Corbett Award as the state's college athlete of the year. In the program for the 1985 event Mulkey was described "as one of the most exciting little packages of dynamite to ever play woman's basketball." Somehow, they forgot to mention the pigtails.

3

Olympics and USA Basketball

While I was playing basketball at Louisiana Tech every summer meant one thing for me—more basketball. After each of my four years, I played for USA Basketball, which is an organization that amasses teams for international competitions that take place all over the world. During those summers, I had a chance to see the world—literally. When I arrived at Louisiana Tech, my entire life experience had pretty much been confined to Louisiana. By the time I left Tech, I had traveled to Europe, South America, and the Far East.

After my freshman year, I tried out for what was then called the Olympic Sports Festival. The Festival was held in Syracuse, New York in 1981 and I was selected to represent the South team. My team ended up winning the gold medal. I can remember one of our victories more than any other because it was against the West team, which included Cheryl Miller and the McGee twins. Cheryl played with such flair and enthusiasm. She was way ahead of her time—a six-foot two-inch perimeter player who could do it all! Although we were usually competing against each other, I still loved how she played the game. She was a star well before her brother Reggie Miller (Indiana Pacers) ever became one. "When we played Kim's team in the festival, I will always remember that she took Cheryl out of her game by constantly talking to her during the entire game," Paula McGee recalls. "They ended up beating us. Kim just rolled Cheryl the entire game with all her talking. Later, I got to know her on one of the USA Basketball teams and she was still the same—competitive, vocal, and always opinionated— like a tiny fireball."

USA Basketball selected a team of players from the four teams represented at the Sports Festival to participate in competitions in Yugoslavia later that summer. I was lucky enough to be chosen for what was called the U.S. Junior National Team. Cheryl Miller and Janice Lawrence, my teammate at Louisiana Tech, were also on the team.

We played a number of games against Yugoslavian teams and won most of them. However, I don't remember much about the games. What I do remember most was the overall experience. It was the first time I traveled outside of the United States. I have a vivid memory of watching a little girl steal bread from a vendor on the street. The vendor chased her down, grabbed her hair, and kicked her until she gave him his bread back. It was a real eye-opening experience for me.

There was also the night when four of us were sleeping in a cabin in the woods. (The entire team was housed in cabins, not in nice hotels like today's athletes.) In the middle of the night, someone tried to open our cabin door. We were scared out of our minds! We were screaming and yelling but never got a response. We couldn't look out the windows because the shutters were locked from the outside. After hours of watching the door handle jiggle, we took the legs off of a table for protection. I declared, "When daylight comes I am opening that door and running for my dear life swinging my table leg." The other players asked how in the world I would know when daylight came. I remembered seeing roosters outside, and being the country girl that I am, I knew they would start crowing at daybreak. Luckily, the person eventually gave up. With the coast clear, we opened the door and sprinted as fast as we could to the coach's cabin. Although we never figured out who it was, we did find liquor bottles everywhere. We assumed the person was intoxicated and just trying to get into the wrong cabin.

After my sophomore year, I was part of a USA Basketball team that played in Europe. Most of the games were played in Eastern European countries, which were still under communist rule. What I remember most about that trip was playing against the Russian center Uljana Semjonova. She stood 7 feet 2 inches tall and I had never seen a woman that tall in my entire life. We beat the Russian team once that summer, something no U.S. women's team had done in years.

During those trips, I was surprised to discover that some women overseas don't shave. It's their culture, I guess, but it was new to me. I'll never forget having to guard a woman that didn't shave; it was so uncomfortable. In addition, they didn't wear the same kind of basketball shorts that we wore. They wore bikini bottoms. Those shorts were a real distraction because they looked so strange to us. I don't think I ever got used to them!

There was so much of the world that I was lucky enough to see. It was amazing and exciting. I saw the best and the worst in a lot of those countries. I saw Red Square and Lenin's Tomb and I kept saying to myself, "I can't believe I'm here."

After my junior year, I visited South America for two events—the World Championships in Brazil and the Pan American Games in Venezuela. It was during the World Championships in Sao Paulo that I had my first opportunity to play for Pat Summitt. She was the head coach at Tennessee and she was going to be the coach of the Olympic team in 1984.

We played two exciting games at the World Championships against the Russian team, and unfortunately, we lost both of them, including the gold-medal game. I was not heartbroken or devastated after either of those two losses. My thinking was, "Okay, so this is their best team and we almost beat them twice." We were so young and hadn't played together for that long. I figured that we would see them again at the Olympics, and if this was the best they had to offer, we were going to be all right. It probably shocked them that we were able to play them so competitively and almost win both games.

The same team then played in the Pan-Am Games with one exception: Pat Summitt wasn't our coach. Instead, Fran Garmon, who coached at Texas Christian University and was Pat's assistant at the Worlds, took over. We weren't nearly as challenged in that tournament because the competition wasn't that strong. We won the gold medal.

I do remember that I played horribly that summer. For some reason I couldn't dribble the ball. I couldn't break a press, which is what I took pride in doing as a player. The ball would bounce off my foot or I would lose control. Maybe I was burned out; I'm not sure. It was incredibly frustrating to play that way. I didn't think, however, that it would hurt my chances terribly of making the Olympic team the next summer. The way I saw it, I just had to get my game fixed before the Louisiana Tech season started. I never lost confidence in my ability and I felt comfortable once I got back to Ruston. I think that summer I just needed a break from basketball.

What I remember most about the Pan Am Games was the village that housed the athletes was never completely finished. The plumbing was dismal. The showers didn't have drainage. Even worse than the plumbing issues was not being able to drink the water during the games. This was the case at both the Pan Am Games and the World Championships. Back then there was no bottled water or Gatorade. We usually drank bottled Cokes, but we couldn't for the games. We were so afraid that we were going to get sick. I took it to the extreme and played games in which I didn't drink a drop of anything. It was only spit and saliva that kept me going. It's astounding that we didn't suffer from severe dehydration on the court or after the games.

The two players I have the most vivid memories of playing against that summer are Semjonova of the Soviet Union and Hortencia Marcari of Brazil, who we played against during the competitions in South America. Semjonova was just so tall. There is a black-and-white photograph of me driving around her and it looks like I only come up to her waist! Hortencia was just a wonderful player. She is considered the greatest women's basketball player in Brazil's history. Both of these players are in the Women's Basketball Hall of Fame and the Naismith Basketball Hall of Fame.

My final experience with USA Basketball was during the 1984 Olympics in Los Angeles. I hoped that I hadn't blown my chance to be on the Olympic team after my awful performance during the NCAA championship game earlier that year. Pat Summitt was watching the game in the stands, but I was hopeful that she had seen enough of me in previous years to know that game was not characteristic of how I could play.

Back then you had to try out for the Olympic team. The tryouts were held a few months after the season ended. It would have been a big disappointment for me not to make that team considering all the time I spent playing for USA Basketball the previous three summers. However, I also knew that there were no gimmes and I wasn't guaranteed to make the team just because of my previous play. I had to perform then and there and it wasn't just for a couple of days. The try-out period went on for a month.

After our last workout, Pat requested a private meeting with each of the remaining players. When she told me I made the Olympic team, I remember trying so hard to keep my composure and hold back my excitement because she hadn't finished meeting with all the players yet. I high-fived her, thanked her, and rushed to the nearest phone to call home with the news. Everyone was ecstatic because making the Olympic team was considered the ultimate achievement. Thinking back today, it is funny to remember all of the players scrambling to find phones to call home with the news—the world before cell phones.

Pat allowed me to return to Louisiana Tech to attend graduation ceremonies. It was a big deal for me to walk across the stage and receive my diploma with my class. I was the first person in my family to earn a college degree and it was an honor for me, as well as for them.

Prior to the Olympics we toured the Far East and participated in what was called the William Jones Cup in Taipei, Taiwan. I was playing as well as I had ever played. I lost a dozen pounds and had new contact lenses. Our team easily won the first four games of the competition. Unfortunately, I woke up one morning and discovered that I couldn't walk. I tried to play in the fifth game, but it was pointless. I sat out the final three games of the competition.

It turned out that I had a stress fracture across the top of my right foot and the only thing you can do for that injury is stay off of it. While the team practiced, I worked out on a stationary bicycle and did some swimming. It was hard not being able to play or practice, and after a while, I even longed for those dreaded suicide drills we had to do at Louisiana Tech. I wanted to get back onto the floor so badly.

When we returned to the United States I had my personal physician in Hammond examine my foot. He confirmed the original diagnosis. My first thought was, "Pat might cut me." This was one of the reasons why they selected alternates. There was still enough time for her to make the switch. The timing could not have been worse. I had played basketball for 10 years and had never been injured. I sprained an ankle once and fractured my finger but those were considered minor injuries. Now, the searing pain wouldn't go away. We tried putting an orthodic in my shoe but that didn't help. There is a difference between being hurt and being injured. And, I was injured. But I knew I had enough time to heal before the Olympics, and soon thereafter, Pat called me and told me, "You made the team. The doctors have convinced me that you'll be good to go come Olympic time. Stay in shape in the water, stay on the stationary bike, and do all you can to be ready to go."

Two weeks prior to the start of the games I was ready to go. By then, however, I had lost the chance to start, but it really didn't matter. I just wanted to play, and when the games were over, I wanted to know I had contributed to the team.

While I was still recovering and on crutches, we played an exhibition game in Indianapolis. It was part of a double-header with the men's Olympic team. The game was the first major sporting event in the new Hoosier Dome in Indianapolis and there were 70,000 people in attendance. The women's team played against a group of former college stars and the men's team played against a group of NBA All-Stars, including Larry Bird of the Boston Celtics. I loved the Celtics during that era. They were my favorite team growing up and Bird was one of my favorite players.

After the women's game ended, I approached Bill Wall, who was in charge of USA Basketball at the time and asked, "Bill, when you see Larry Bird come out of the locker room, you have got to introduce me to him." All I wanted to do was meet him. That's not normally like me but when would I ever get the chance to meet Larry Bird again?

When he finally came out for the game, I went down and sat next to him on the bench. Right away he started needling me. I was just flabbergasted that he even knew who I was. He started picking on me, making smart remarks about how I missed that last shot against Southern California in the NCAA championship game. He didn't have to say another thing to me. I just sat there astounded thinking, "Wow, he watched that game." I found out later that Larry is a big fan of the women's game.

After the game, I joined Larry, Kevin McHale, and Quinn Buckner as they walked back to the hotel, me hobbling along on my crutches. I'm sure it's something Larry doesn't even remember, but it's something I'll never forget. There wasn't much of a conversation, however, because cars were stopping alongside the road, people were honking their horns, and fans were yelling out their car windows to Larry. I was caught up in the moment thinking, "Here I am, walking down the street with three NBA stars!"

In 2005, when we drove to the RCA Dome during the Final Four, I looked out the window of our team bus and that was one of the things I thought about—walking back to the hotel on my crutches and getting a chance to speak to an idol of mine—Larry Bird.

The Olympic team or any USA Basketball team has a totally different composition than a college team. There is all this talent compacted into one team, with so many egos as opposed to just a few. In addition, the international game is different from what I was used to. But all of it was good fun for me. As a point guard, all I had to do was make sure that we were in the right offense, the right defense, and that I made the first pass to get us into our offense. I think back on that team and, wow, did we have some talent. We had Cheryl Miller, Lynnette Woodard, Anne Donovan, and Janice Lawrence along with Lea

Henry, Teresa Edwards, Carol Menken-Schaudt, Pamela McGee, Denise Curry, Cindy Noble, and Cathy Boswell. I loved playing with Cheryl. I enjoyed her style and her enthusiasm. We played the same way. I'd get fired up, high-five, chest-butt. I'd do all that stuff. There was never any friction whatsoever between us. At that age, we were young adults and all we were focused on was winning the gold medal. That team would still do very well today. We had size, shooters, athletes, and we were smart players.

The opening ceremony was at the Los Angeles Memorial Coliseum and it was an incredible experience walking into that stadium with the rest of the U.S. delegation. We had to wait an awful long time because the host nation is the last one introduced. But it was still worth it. We could see all the movie stars in the stands. I remember seeing John Forsythe and Linda Evans from *Dynasty* as we were walking into the stadium.

I have wonderful memories of that summer. We had such a good team. The only downside was that the Russians boycotted the Olympic Games that year. I'm not sure it would have mattered, though. We were so good we probably would have beaten them anyway. We never lost a game and I still vividly remember standing on the podium receiving the gold medal. I sang the entire national anthem with tears in my eyes—and I can't even carry a tune! The thought in my head was, "This is the end and what a way to go out!" It was the culmination of all we had worked for and we went out on top. I knew my sneakers would be on the shelf forever. There would be no more basketball for me!

One of my most vivid memories of the Olympics didn't even involve a game or a player from our own team. One day, we were on the team bus driving back to the Olympic Village after a practice and we drove past a man walking in the same direction wearing all this USA Basketball gear. It wasn't a particularly good section of Los Angeles and we wondered what was going on. We rolled down the windows of the team bus to get a closer look. Then, Cheryl Miller exclaimed, "It's Leon Wood. It's Leon Wood." Leon was on the men's Olympic team, a guard from Cal State-Fullerton. Coach Bob Knight had thrown him out of practice and ordered him to walk back to the Olympic Village. We offered him a ride on our bus, but he wouldn't take it. "That man told me to walk back to the village and I'm going to walk back to the village," he said. We all roared. Today, Leon is a referee in the NBA.

After the Olympics, the medal-winning athletes were taken on a tour of several U.S. cities. We met President Reagan in Washington, DC, had a ticker-tape parade in New York City with Mayor Ed Koch, and went to see a Dallas Cowboys football game. Those gatherings represented the best—and sometimes the only—chance for me to meet some of the other Olympic athletes, individuals I didn't get to see that much of during the games. I enjoyed spending time with people like Mary Lou Retton, Rowdy Gaines, Evander Holyfield, the players from the men's team including Patrick Ewing and Michael Jordan.

Soon after the Olympics ended, I flew back to Ruston and picked up my brand new white Corvette, which was a gift from my parents for my college graduation. Mary Belle Tuten and I began the four-hour drive home to Hammond, where festivities were planned in my honor. We were 30 miles from Hammond, when a policeman on the side of the interstate pulled me over. However, I wasn't speeding or doing anything wrong. When the police officer approached me, I noticed he was from the Tangiphoa Parish Sheriff's Department and he was holding a bouquet of red roses for me! Mary Belle and I were given a police escort the rest of the way to Hammond. As we approached town, my sister, Tammy, flagged down our car and switched places with Mary Belle, so she could ride by my side during the celebration parade through Hammond. I was wearing the Olympic gold medal around my neck during the parade, but I remember at one point taking it off and putting it around my sister's neck. She was extremely touched by the gesture.

There was one celebration after another over that summer. The town of Tickfaw had a parade and named a street in my honor: Kim Mulkey Drive. I remember getting the key to the city of Hammond and there being a lot of officials and dignitaries at all the events. I even remember cutting a ribbon at the opening of a McDonald's restaurant with Ronald McDonald standing next to me— a child's dream come true.

There was a plaque placed in the ground in my honor at City Hall in Hammond. The plaque reads: "We proudly recognize Kim Mulkey for the honor she brought to the United States and the city of Hammond. Her outstanding athletic ability and team spirit was demonstrated in winning the gold medal in women's basketball at the 1984 Summer Olympic Games." I've been asked a lot about the plaque and I always say the same thing—it reminds me of a gravestone!

I hope some day to be able to have the honor of coaching a team for USA Basketball. When my kids are older, off to college, and on their own, I really hope I get the opportunity. USA Basketball asked me if I would be interested in coaching the Under 20 women in the FIBA Americas tournament in 2006. The tournament was being held in Mexico City in early August, but I couldn't do it. However, I did beg USA Basketball to keep me on its list of coaches for the future because I really want the opportunity someday. I feel like it's a way to give back to the game, especially at the international level. Those experiences were priceless and invaluable to me.

4

The Coaching Life

In the spring of 1984 I graduated from Louisiana Tech and was awarded a $2,000 post-graduate scholarship by the NCAA. It was a tremendous honor, because at the time I received it, it was only awarded to five male and five female college athletes in the United States. Still awarded today, the scholarship honors student athletes who excel both academically and athletically.

Playing more basketball wasn't an option for me after graduation and I had no interest in coaching. From my perspective, what else was there for me to do? I had accomplished everything I wanted to on the basketball court. If an opportunity had interested me I might have explored it, but the idea of going overseas to play in order to make money didn't excite me. Moreover, there was no need for me over there—people my size are a dime a dozen overseas. I had no intention of remaining in basketball.

So, scholarship in hand I decided to remain in Ruston and earn an MBA in business administration. My undergraduate degree was in general business and I somehow envisioned myself working for a big company, flying around the world in a corporate jet. I even had thoughts of possibly pursuing a law degree or entering public service.

As I was working on my master's degree Sonja Hogg had an idea. She went to President Taylor and suggested that I join Coach Barmore's staff as an assistant. "I was in the process of a separation and I was ready to do something different," Hogg explains. "Dr. Taylor pleaded with me not to leave. But I told him that I wanted to go, but we needed to do something first. We needed to leave some people around Leon who could help him recruit and help him keep things together." Hogg continues, "I told him that Kim should be one of those people. She had just returned from the Olympics where she won the gold medal. She was probably the most popular player we'd ever had at Tech. I thought we should hire her as an assistant coach and put her in charge of the recruiting." Hogg says today, "I told Dr. Taylor that if we put the right people in place Louisiana Tech would continue to roll. At the time, that is what Tech needed. And there was no way he was going to let that program go down the tubes."

Sure enough, a few months into my graduate studies Dr. Taylor approached me and expressed that he wanted me to join Coach Barmore's staff. I succinctly told him that I wasn't interested. He said, "What if Leon talks to you because I've told him I want you on his staff?" Well, I knew how that worked. I said to myself, "He wants a female who loves the program, is committed to it, and has a recognizable name and face." He knew I understood Coach Barmore as well as anyone, but no coach wants to hire someone just because the college president tells him to. I knew how much Dr. Taylor loved the program and that his intentions were good, but I felt uncomfortable with him asking me to join Coach Barmore's staff. As a head coach you want to hire your own people.

Nevertheless, Coach Barmore approached me directly and convinced me that he really wanted me to join his staff. He said he hadn't come to me earlier because he thought I didn't want to coach. He was right—I didn't. I had played for the man for four years and I thought it was time for me to move on to something different. But he was convincing and we ended up sharing 15 wonderful years of coaching together. "Kim was worshipped in Ruston. How could I find anyone better? She knew exactly what we needed to stay in the ballgame," Barmore says today. "She was a tough athlete who didn't hesitate to get down and dirty on the floor and work up a sweat. Nevertheless, off the floor she was very much a lady."

I don't know why I didn't originally consider becoming a coach. On some level, I might have thought that the financial reward would be greater in the business world. Whatever the reason, I'm glad that I changed my mind because coaching is truly what I was meant to do. It comes so naturally to me. I thank God that F. Jay Taylor, Leon Barmore, and Sonja Hogg convinced me to coach—look what I would have been missing!

"Kim's job at the outset was recruiting and academics," Barmore says. "She would go out and find 'em. And then she would keep 'em eligible. She knew every professor at Tech and she stayed on top of those kids academically. That was huge for us because some of the kids were a challenge. We weren't Stanford or Harvard. We had to take some borderline kids. There were places we went recruiting which weren't the best places and it meant something to a parent to have Kim look them in the eye and say, 'I will make sure your daughter stays academically eligible.' You couldn't promise that at a big university, but Kim could promise it at Tech. We were at the top of the heap back then and our goal was to keep us there."

To this day, one thing I take a lot of pride in is that while I was in charge of academics at Louisiana Tech not one player ever became academically ineligible. I meant it when I told families that I would look out for their daughters both athletically and academically.

Coach Barmore didn't like to travel very far when we were trying to recruit a player. One year I convinced him to fly with me to Oregon. We needed a point guard and there was a player named Laurie Milligan who I thought would be a terrific fit for our program. Before going on a trip like this I always did my homework. I knew our strengths and weaknesses at Louisiana Tech and I was prepared for any question that might come up. The night before our visit there was a fire in our motel and I can remember Coach Barmore saying, "This had better be worth it."

Barmore recalls Dick Milligan, Laurie's father, having a long list of questions about Louisiana Tech. "What was the graduation rate? What was the average class size? All that kind of stuff," Barmore says. "Kim had the answers for him. She didn't say, 'I'll check on that and get back to you.' She didn't say, 'I don't know, but I'll find out.' She knew every answer. It was amazing."

Dick Milligan remembers something else that Mulkey said during their visit. "She didn't make any promises to Laurie about playing time, but Kim did say she would take Laurie under her wing, she would mentor her, she would work with her, she would do everything she could to help Laurie achieve the same kind of success that she had at Louisiana Tech," Dick recalls. "As a parent that was thrilling for me to hear. They didn't have to say another word. As far as I was concerned, Laurie was theirs."

Alas, Laurie Milligan ended up going to Tennessee, the only other college she seriously considered. To this day, she is the only college player, male or female, to have played in four consecutive Division I NCAA championship basketball games.

When I started coaching there was no one to teach me how to recruit, so I taught myself. I soon discovered that the key to recruiting is being able to identify the right player for your team and system. I had a pretty good knack for it because I was so familiar with the Lady Techsters and Coach Barmore.

I would attend AAU tournaments in the summer and watch hundreds of kids play. I would try to find that right player. I'd start by examining Tech's needs. Did we need a certain position player? Did we need to go for depth at a certain position? Did we need better shooters? Did we need to get quicker? Or taller? Was there some can't-miss player out there who we had to have? We mostly recruited local kids who were familiar with Louisiana Tech's program and tradition. We also tried to be smart and only recruit players that we felt we had a real shot at signing. By all means, we weren't going to travel around the country just to say we were in on this kid or that kid.

Coach Barmore used to say that I was a lot like him, maybe too much like him, and this was evident when we recruited a player. The way he looked at it was if Louisiana Tech wasn't one of the recruit's top three choices then the heck with it. Maybe we were too impatient in that regard, but that's how we both felt. His one overriding concern: control the State of Louisiana. In other words, if there was a Division I recruit in the state whom we felt could play for Louisiana Tech we had better be able to sign her.

I remember two distinct times when we fell short of recruiting instate talent. I tried to recruit former LSU coach Pokey Chatman out of Hahnville High School in 1987. She was a terrific high school point guard, but she ended up going to LSU. Another Louisiana prospect that we wanted and didn't get was Alana Beard, who played for Southwood High School in Shreveport. I worked harder to get her than any other player I ever recruited. Nevertheless, I could never even convince her to visit Louisiana Tech. She wanted to go to Duke and that was that. That's when I realized that times were starting to change and we didn't always get the best Louisiana kids. More schools were emphasizing women's basketball and more women were going to the so-called "academic" institutions. We would never have lost a player like Alana in the early 1980s.

"Other than Pokey and Alana, the rest of them, we usually got," says Barmore. "[Kim] also got Shantel Hardison, who was from Natchitoches," Barmore says. "She was a Gatorade Player of the Year in 1988. We already had a commitment from her when I heard that she might change her mind and go to LSU. I said, 'Kim, you go back down there and do whatever you have to do to make sure that girl comes to Tech.' And that girl came to Tech. Very seldom did Kim lose a player in the state of Louisiana."

I remember how I felt the first time a recruit rejected me. I cried like a baby. I had spent so much time and effort recruiting her that I couldn't imagine her turning me down. Her name was Carmen Davis and she lived with her grandmother in Memphis, Tennessee. When we went to visit her Coach Barmore, who is a big Elvis Presley fan, discovered that Carmen's grandmother was once one of

Elvis' cooks at Graceland. Well, that made the trip for him. But despite the Elvis connection, we just couldn't close the deal with Carmen and she ended up going to Georgia Tech.

You soon learn that rejection is part of it. Some recruits you get without working that hard and others you get because you put in the extra time and effort. Still others you don't get no matter how much extra you put into it. You can never really know what makes a young woman make a decision. It can be connections to a school. It can be playing time or the position she'll play. It can be her relationship with the coach or her relationship with her boyfriend and where he's going. You just never know. Coach Barmore always said if a player didn't sign with us it wasn't necessarily the recruiter's fault.

In addition, sometimes Louisiana Tech was a hard sell. If you lived in or around Ruston or were familiar with the Lady Techsters then we had a good chance of signing you as a recruit. But Ruston didn't appeal to everyone. Coach Barmore used to tell me that he had two options when he drove a recruit around Ruston. If the young lady was from a big city he would take a number of different roads, weaving in and around the town in order to create the illusion that Ruston was a bigger place than it was. If the recruit was from a small town, he would simply drive her down the main street and point out all the buildings and stores.

There were some other interesting recruiting trips over the years. One time Kristy Curry, who was also an assistant, and I went to see a junior college post player in Tallahassee, Florida. Kristy thought we had to drive, but I told her that we were flying this time. She figured we were traveling on a Lear jet or something. Not quite. F. Jay Taylor's wife, Lou, piloted us in her little private plane. We made it, but Kristy was very pale the entire time we were in the air. Those were the kinds of trips we had to make back then. Curry, now the head coach at Texas Tech, recalls the trip saying, "The airplane was one of those ones you see people flying on Sundays to sightsee. I had to sit on a water cooler the whole trip and I was trying hard not to get sick because you always wanted to look strong in front of Kim. That's because she was so strong."

Curry also recalls that Mulkey had a voracious appetite. "That woman loved to eat and she ate well," she said. Jennifer Roberts, a student manager, concurs with Curry. "Kim could never wait for lunch. We used to go to this place called The Rib Shack. It was a hole in the wall barbecue joint and Kim would always get these huge baked potatoes loaded with butter, cheese, the works. She loved the place."

I also enjoyed eating at a restaurant in Ruston called the Blue Light. It had terrific soul food and was the epitome of informal dining. All the booths and tables had numbers. Once you found a seat, which could be pretty difficult at lunchtime, you would decide what you wanted to eat by reading a menu written on the wall. Orders were placed at the main counter by writing it, along with your seat number, on a blank piece of paper. Soon enough, your food was delivered to your table.

Coach Barmore is only 18 years older than I am, but I have always characterized our relationship as being like that of a father and daughter. We would cry. We would fight. We would hug. There was no assistant more loyal to him than I was. I fought so many battles for him and with him. To this day, I refer to Leon Barmore as Coach Barmore. I think it shows a sign of respect.

I don't ever remember signing a contract at Louisiana Tech. You worked at the pleasure of the head coach. I know Coach Barmore told me that he never signed more than a one-year deal until the early 1990s when former NFL receiver Jerry Stovall became the athletic director and signed him to a multi-year contract. Now, of course, contracts are standard.

I remember Coach Barmore trying to throw some extra money my way over the years. He would always find a way to pay me for the camps we held each summer. He didn't want me to leave Tech and I was happy to remain where I was. Mary Belle Tuten always likes to say that I'm a nester and she's probably right. I was settled and comfortable living in Ruston.

My coaching responsibilities soon evolved beyond recruiting and academics. I worked with the guards, which included all the perimeter players. Our drills focused on passing, defending, proper positioning, shooting—the whole nine yards. At staff meetings Coach

Barmore would tell me what he wanted and I would go out there and get it done. I knew exactly what he wanted because I had played for the man for four years and he had taught me the very same things.

When I first started coaching I still approached our relationship from the player-coach perspective. I'd wonder, "How do I say this to him? How do I approach him with that?" But the older I got, the more responsibility I received. The longer we were together, the more loyalty we showed each other. Each year I became a little bit braver. Eventually, I became comfortable saying what I felt even when I knew it might upset him or he might disagree. Over time I felt that I could say whatever I wanted about Coach Barmore—and no one else could—because I just loved the guy. I knew his strengths, his weaknesses, and his faults. Through the years, as is the case in many father-daughter relationships, I became more willing to challenge him, to speak out, and to battle him on issues that I felt strongly about. Those issues ranged from recruiting to day-to-day stuff, but most of the time they were nothing really major.

One of the sports writers in Ruston used to kid me about being Coach Barmore's "coattail holder," for lack of a better phrase. Coach Barmore would sometimes get on the officials something fierce; he would even try to go out on the court and argue his point. That is a definite no-no. As his lead assistant I would jump up and hold his sports coat from the back so he couldn't go out on the floor and get called for a technical foul. There's no telling how many times I saved him.

Coach Barmore would ask me to compile scouting reports on our next opponent, which was the kind of attention-to-detail work that I really liked. It was like being back in school, going over game tape again and again trying to pick out certain tendencies of another team. I would pop a tape into my office VCR, plop my feet up onto my desk, grab the remote control, and go to work. I know it's a lot more sophisticated these days but that was how I did it back then. Even today when I am studying a game tape in my office I will sometimes find myself in the same intense mode—feet propped up on my desk, remote control in hand.

"If I gave Kim an assignment on Monday and told her I needed it on Friday, she would have it for me on Tuesday," Barmore recalls. "I really came to rely on her for my scouting reports. They were incredibly detailed. I always wanted her to detail the top five sets of the other team so we knew what they were going to run and wouldn't get beaten by anything unfamiliar." Barmore says today, "If I asked for the top five sets. Kim would give me 20. We'd go through the five they used the most and I'd say, 'That's fine.' But Kim would always say, 'One more, Coach. One more.' So maybe we'd do one more. Now, if I saw something that was new to me in the game and that had not been covered, well, I'm the head coach. And what does the head coach do? He blames the assistants. So, of course, we played this one game and in the second half the opponent ran this play I had never seen. I glared at Kim. She looked back and didn't say anything, except 'One more, Coach.' After the game, I asked her for her scouting report, and sure enough, there was the set that I hadn't recognized right there in the scouting report."

My first offer or interest in a head coaching position came from the University of South Carolina in 1987. I made a visit and thoroughly enjoyed it. However, I had only been an assistant coach for a couple of years and I felt I just wasn't ready. I still needed to learn more from Coach Barmore.

In 1988, I visited the University of Missouri. Joe Castiglione, now the athletic director at Oklahoma, is one of my favorite people in the business. He was the athletic director at Missouri back then. As much as I would have enjoyed working with Joe, I just couldn't see myself so far away from my roots.

A decade later I was contacted by Texas A&M University about an opening there. This job opportunity was really exciting considering College Station, Texas was much closer to my roots than either Columbia, Missouri or Columbia, South Carolina. In addition, Lynn Hickey, the senior women's administrator at Texas A&M at the time, was one of my coaches for USA Basketball in 1982. The offer was really tempting. I felt that the school was ready to seriously commit to women's basketball and they sold me on everything. I can't explain why I didn't take the job. The money was great. The conference was good, but I didn't do it. My comfort zone was at Louisiana Tech.

After turning down these offers I never got more money from Louisiana. When I went on those visits the result was one of two things: take the new job or come back to my old job. I believe Coach Barmore would have given me the moon if he could have, but he didn't have the resources. Before the start of the 1996–97 basketball season Coach Barmore was able to promote me to associate head coach. It was a change in title and a little more money, but essentially, my job stayed pretty much the same.

In 1997, the WNBA was starting its first season and one of the teams, the Houston Comets, was interested in hiring Coach Barmore. I know there was a lot of talk back and forth between Coach Barmore and Carroll Dawson, the general manager of the Comets. Coach Barmore told me that he came close to accepting the job.

I was kept abreast of the situation and I suppose I was thinking on some level that if Coach Barmore accepted the job I would be the logical candidate to succeed him. But I knew deep down that Coach Barmore would never leave Louisiana Tech. Ruston was his home. He was so powerful there, why would he ever want to leave?

Tech's success on the court continued as I started my coaching career. We went to the NCAA championship game in my second season as an assistant, but we lost to Tennessee. We beat Tennessee in the semifinals the following year and went on to beat Auburn in the championship game. It was my first championship as an assistant and I know it remains Coach Barmore's personal favorite.

We advanced to the NCAA championship game twice more while I was on Coach Barmore's staff and lost both times. The first loss to North Carolina in 1994 remains one of the most painful experiences of my coaching life. We had a two-point lead with less than one second to play. In fact, there was seven-tenths—0.7—of a second remaining. North Carolina had the ball under their basket and we were in a man-to-man defense. Two of our players got confused about what they were supposed to do on a screen. One switched. One did not. Charlotte Smith was open and the inbound passer spotted her and was able to get her the ball. Charlotte nailed the three pointer. I was three months pregnant at the time and I literally thought I was going to miscarry right there on the sideline—the pain was that intense. It was the most gut-wrenching feeling I have ever felt in coaching.

In what turned out to be my last year at Louisiana Tech I was itching to become a head coach. Coach Barmore and I talked about the interest I had received from other programs. He said to me, "Kim, I'm not going to sign another contract at Louisiana Tech. You're the heir apparent. This is where you need to be." I told him, "I know it coach."

Not much later I picked up the morning newspaper and read that Coach Barmore had signed a five-year contract extension. It was August. I thought to myself, "This is strange. We've got such a good relationship. Why didn't he tell me? Why did I have to read about it in the newspaper?"

I called his home and his wife, Rachel, answered. Coach Barmore wasn't home, so I asked her to deliver my congratulations. I also told her that I wasn't going to be another Bill Guthridge. (Bill was the longtime assistant coach to Dean Smith at North Carolina who eventually got the head job, but didn't last long.) I made up my mind that I wasn't going to stay around Louisiana Tech forever waiting for Coach Barmore to leave.

Coach Barmore called me back and said, "We'll talk soon. I'll explain it then." I replied, "Coach, you don't have to explain anything. You're a legend here. You can stay as long as you want. But I can't." When Coach Barmore and I finally got together he told me that he signed a new contract to help with his retirement package. I said, "That's fine. I just want you to know that you could have told me. What kind of relationship do we really have?"

Prior to the start of the season, there was an incident between Coach Barmore and myself that resulted in my stepping away from the program for a few days. One of the things that he was adamant about was never embarrassing his assistant coaches in front of the players. An assistant has no credibility if the head coach criticizes them in front of the players. The players will lose respect if they see it. Well, that's what he did one day. He made a comment about me in front of the team that stunned and humiliated me. The players were baffled. I walked away, thinking to myself, "Well, this is it." I thought at the time that I was finished coaching at Louisiana Tech. I asked President Dan Reneau if he would keep me on salary and transfer me to another department until the end of the year. At the end of the season I would find another coaching job. President Reneau agreed. Coach Barmore and I did not connect for those few days, but when we finally did he was overly apologetic. He knew what he had done was wrong and he felt horrible about it. He was very sincere in his apology and he asked me to come back, so I did. I know that Coach Barmore genuinely loves me and I love him. I came back with the intention of finishing the year and I did.

Coach Barmore surprised me once again at the end of that season. In March, he announced out of the clear blue that he was retiring at the end of the upcoming season. He didn't tell anybody and no one saw it coming. I know he did it to keep me from going anywhere because it was time for me to be a head coach. I am forever grateful for that. I looked at him and said, "You're not ready to retire. You're only 55 years old. You've still got a lot of coaching left in you."

A couple of days later Coach Barmore asked me if I had heard anything from the Louisiana Tech administration concerning the soon-to-be-available job. I told him that I had not. He was incredulous. He said, "Are you telling me that you haven't heard a word from them? They haven't contacted you about the job?" I told him that was exactly what I was saying.

A few weeks passed and we advanced to the NCAA Tournament. I still hadn't heard a thing. During this time, the athletic director was quoted in the newspaper saying that Louisiana Tech was conducting a national search for Coach Barmore's replacement. Well, that hit me like a ton of bricks.

I never considered calling the president or athletic director to ask them about the job. I felt that I had proven myself loyal by turning down three head coaching jobs. I had been at that university and a part of the Lady Techster program for 19 years. I was no stranger to them; they knew where to find me.

Also during this time I became aware of Baylor University's interest. Coach Barmore told me that the university had called and was interested in talking to me about its head coaching position. Carroll Dawson, the general manager of the NBA Houston Rockets and the WNBA Houston Comets, was the one to initiate the call. As a proud alumnus and former basketball coach at the university, he was acting as an emissary of sorts for Baylor. Coach Barmore told Dawson that he thought I would be an excellent candidate for Baylor but I was probably not going to be available because Louisiana Tech was going to offer me the head coaching job.

Baylor called again during the NCAA Tournament, but it was mostly a general call letting me know that they were following Louisiana Tech's progress. Tom Stanton, the athletic director, did ask if I thought he should move on to someone else because Louisiana Tech was eventually going to offer me the job. I informed him Louisiana

Tech had not said a word to me about succeeding Leon. This was weeks after Coach Barmore had announced his intention to retire. Tom Stanton responded, "You've got to be kidding."

Newspaper readers were told something quite different. Before the team left for Kansas City and the Midwest regional tournament, a story came across the Associated Press wire saying that I was offered the head coaching job at Louisiana Tech. The story went on to say that I had agreed to wait until the end of the season before making a final decision. None of that was true. The story contained a quote from the chairman of the Louisiana Tech Athletics Council saying, "We recommended her for the job and we hope that she takes it. We have faith in her that she can take our program forward and we hope she does." The athletics council is a group of faculty and alumni that acts as a board of directors, conducting interviews and making hiring recommendations. There was even a salary referenced in the story, although there was no mention of the length of the supposed offer. At that point I had never met with the Louisiana Tech Athletics Council—and, I never did.

In the 2000 NCAA Tournament, we lost to Penn State in the Midwest regional finals at Kansas City. We got absolutely crushed, 86–65. I got back to the hotel and my phone was ringing. It was Tom Stanton asking me if I would come to visit Baylor. I said, "How quickly can you get a plane here?"

Before I visited Baylor, I finally heard from Louisiana Tech. It was obvious to me that someone had told them of my intent to visit Baylor. I called Tom Stanton and told him I would still make a visit, but he needed to know that Louisiana Tech had finally called and I was going to meet with the school president and athletic director to hear what they had to say.

When I finally sat down for my first meeting with Dan Reneau and Jim Oakes I was expecting that they would at least talk about the job, but the topic never came up. It was a very general meeting. We talked about joining the Western Athletic Conference and how whoever followed Coach Barmore was going to have to be tough because he was such a legend. There was a big elephant in the room and everyone was avoiding it. We talked and talked, but we never got anywhere. When the meeting ended I informed them that I was heading to Baylor because they had offered me a job and I was going to see what it entailed.

I knew nothing—absolutely nothing—about Baylor. The only thing I knew about Waco was that the Branch Davidian disaster had happened there years earlier and Sonja Hogg was their head coach, but she was resigning at the end of the season. I had been to Waco once before but never visited the Baylor campus. I vaguely recalled that we beat Baylor when I was a sophomore at Louisiana Tech and we beat them again in a holiday tournament in Shreveport when I was an assistant coach. That was it, though. And I had to reach way back in my memory to even recall those games.

It was the timing as much as it was anything. They were pursuing me at a time when I finally decided I might be ready to leave Louisiana Tech. I wasn't aspiring to live in Texas or coach in the Big 12 Conference. It was nothing like that. They were the school that happened to be on the line when I was ready and willing to listen.

I told Tom Stanton that I would make a commitment to him that I would come to Baylor to visit but only if he was going to offer me the job. I would not come and be one of 10 candidates interviewed because I felt that Louisiana Tech would eventually offer me the position. We didn't talk about a contract or money.

My husband and I flew to Waco and Tom Stanton met us at the airport. He took us around the campus, introduced us to school officials, and told us what a great family town Waco was. He made sure that Randy was involved in all the meetings. I can remember standing on a street corner and looking around at all these various restaurants and knowing right then and there that Waco was very different from Ruston.

After the tour, Tom took us to a conference room at the Hilton and we talked for four hours. He made it clear that the job was mine if I wanted it. He mentioned all the upgrades and improvements he had in mind for the program. He envisioned hiring not just coaches, but also leaders and he saw that leadership quality in me. He saw me as more than a coach down the road; he saw me as a real long-term asset to the university. He was sick of Baylor being a training ground for coaches who would move on to bigger and better jobs; he wanted the school to be a place where coaches stayed for the long haul.

He knew it was hard for me because I was so entrenched at Louisiana Tech—and I was. I still hadn't made up my mind even with his offer on the table. It was everything I wanted, both in terms of money and security. It was a better package than I would ever get at Louisiana Tech, but I am sometimes loyal to a fault and I felt an extreme amount of loyalty to the Lady Techster program.

But I was torn. I was still waiting to hear from Louisiana Tech. But I couldn't stop thinking about a question that Tom Stanton posed to me. He asked, "Do you want to be seen as a caretaker at Louisiana Tech, following in the footsteps of a giant like Leon Barmore, or do you want to make a mark in the industry by building something all your own, basically from scratch?" He also pointed out to me that the way college athletics was evolving, Louisiana Tech would never be as powerful as it once was. Baylor, on the other hand, was in the Big 12 Conference with more resources. While I was impressed and flattered I couldn't give him an answer right then and there. He understood and asked that I go home and think about it. I think he appreciated that I was up front and candid with him about the pull that Louisiana Tech still had on me. When you spend 38 years of your life in one state and 19 years of your life at one university your heart is just aching. I always felt I'd stay at Louisiana Tech. There was no negotiation in terms of Baylor giving me more money or anything like that. I just said, "Tom, if Louisiana Tech gives me a five-year deal, I'm staying. But if you'll be patient with me, it doesn't look like that is going to happen."

After returning from Waco with an offer in hand from Baylor, I called Jim Oakes. Jim was a good guy, but Dan Reneau was the one who held all the power. I had promised Jim that I would call him when I got back and I did, pulling over at Southern Maid Donuts in Shreveport just after I landed.

The first question out of Jim's mouth was, "Did they offer you the job?" I said, "Jim, I told you before I left that I wouldn't have gone there if they weren't going to offer me the job." I expressed that I would not stay at Louisiana Tech for anything less than five years. I didn't expect them to pay me what Baylor could pay me—that wasn't realistic and I've never been about money. What was important to me was the five years.

First, five years would give me 20 years in the state's retirement system. Second, it was going to be my first head-coaching job and I was going to be following a legend, a future Hall of Famer. Five years was important to me, because if I was going to turn down the type of money Baylor offered me, wouldn't it be reasonable to get some type of security? I thought that was fair. It's the standard in the business. Security was all I wanted.

While going through the decision process, Randy and I had some close friends over to the house one night to talk it over with them. Randy produced a spreadsheet of sorts to show all of us why it was best that I should not turn down this opportunity. He had calculated the numbers to show how much money I would make and how much money he would make with all the new opportunities.

I needed some wise counsel, so I talked with Mary Belle Tuten who was a member of the Athletics Council at that time. She didn't understand why Louisiana Tech had not stepped up and offered me the job, but she offered the following great advice: take a job where the people really want you because you deserve at least that much. At the time, neither one of us felt that Louisiana Tech had shown that they really wanted me.

Mary Belle also reminded me that there would be a huge difference between the programs at Baylor and Louisiana Tech. Baylor, a private university, could offer more money, bigger budgets, and better facilities than Louisiana Tech, a state school. She told me, "You won't ever worry about your recruiting budget or your travel budget at Baylor. You won't have to worry about replacing a filing cabinet at Baylor."

With Louisiana Tech about to join the Western Athletic Conference recruiting and travel would loom large. The conference included teams like Hawaii, Fresno State, Idaho, and Nevada. Geographically, the travel would be extensive.

Jim and I had another meeting and this time the job came up for discussion. I was offered a three-year deal. I said, "Jim, c'mon, no." Then they came back with a four-year deal. There were other things discussed like camp issues. I could make extra money from basketball camps in the summer, but all of it was, in my mind, trivial and not central to the point. It was the five years. I told him again that I would not stay at Louisiana Tech without a five-year deal.

During this time, I was in constant contact with Coach Barmore, seeking his advice and counsel. He totally supported my position although he also felt that in the end the school would take care of me. He made it clear that he wanted me to be his successor.

There was one final meeting with the president and the athletic director in the president's office on the top floor of Wyly Tower. I went through every feeling imaginable as I tried to convince the president to give me what I wanted. I got out of my chair, onto my knees, and begged that man for a five-year contract. Tears were flying everywhere. It was humiliating. I was a strong-willed woman who had never done anything like that in her entire life. I was trying to show him the passion I had for the university, the program. How could he not appreciate the loyalty I had shown them? Three different times I had turned down higher paying jobs to stay at Louisiana Tech. Give the girl what she wants!

When I was at that man's knees he had the coldest look in his eyes. I tried to make it easier on him. I said, "If you can't do it in writing just verbally tell me that you'll give me the fifth year and we'll shake on it." Dan Reneau looked at me and said, "I will guarantee you a fifth year in some capacity at this university." I thought to myself, "What does that mean? Does that mean that I'm going to mop the floors in Memorial Gymnasium for that last year?"

I don't know what his reasoning was and I haven't had a conversation with him since. Coach Barmore thinks it was simply two strong-willed people, both excellent in their chosen fields, unable to reach an agreement. I know that Dr. Taylor, the former president of the school, was in my corner and made his opinion known, but after 25 years in the position he retired in 1987. While still influential around Ruston, he did not have the absolute power anymore. If he did, I doubt I would have left—and neither does he.

When Louisiana State's longtime coach Sue Gunter retired LSU handled it correctly by giving her assistant, Pokey Chatman, the job. Pokey had spent as many years at LSU as I had at Louisiana Tech. In my mind it was an absolute no-brainer. If you're the athletic director you walk down the hall and ask, "Sue Gunter, who do you want?" She replies, "Pokey Chatman." End of conversation. I don't know if Pokey got a five-year contract but what was clear is that Louisiana State acted as if they wanted her as soon as Sue Gunter announced her retirement. There was absolutely no suspense. They handled it beautifully, just the way it should have been.

I'd spent 19 years at one university as a player and a coach and I didn't feel like I had to prove myself to anyone. They knew my loyalty. They knew I'd been a Louisiana kid all my life and that I'd just built my dream house on four acres of land. Look at my resume. What else could I do? What else did I need to do to get a five-year deal? I wasn't even looking for them to put it in writing. All they had to do was verbalize the commitment to a fifth year and I would have taken the deal. I just wanted Dan Reneau to say, "Hey Kim, you know we'll take care of you, you're one of us." But the man was so cold.

I begged him to let me meet with the Athletics Council and explain to them why a five-year deal was so important to me. I thought that maybe the council could influence the president, even though the president is entitled to the final decision because he is the president.

It dawned on me right then and there—as I knelt before him begging—your gut never lies. My gut was saying, "Something's not right here." I had always lived my life trying to do the right thing. I'd been loyal. I'd been dedicated. I'd given everything I had to playing for and coaching at Louisiana Tech. There was nothing else I could have done to prove to them that I deserved a five-year commitment. It was time to go. I got up off my knees, left the room, and I never looked back. I called Tom Stanton and told him that I was going to take the job.

Looking back, I don't know why Dan Reneau did what he did, but today, I thank him. One of my favorite sayings is "thank God for unanswered prayers." I would have never left and realized that there was another world out there. I was blinded by my loyalty to one school and one state. Regardless of where my career takes me, Louisiana will always be my home. It took something very negative for me to leave Louisiana Tech but there was some other place in need of my loyalty and dedication.

When I announced I was leaving, Louisiana Tech sent out a press release with all these lies about shoe contract money and other issues that had never even been discussed. I called Jim Oakes and said, "Shame on you." He said it didn't come from his office. That is all he needed to say for me to know exactly where it came from. The public relations department had written it at the bequest of the president's office.

All the release needed to say was that I wanted a five-year deal and that Dan Reneau didn't think I was worthy of it. End of story. They didn't need to make it look like they offered me all this money and incentives. They tried to make me look petty and greedy. My opinion is that it was a power move. The president wasn't going to give into me because he had given into Coach Barmore's demands for all those years. Coach Barmore was an institution at Louisiana Tech. Coach Barmore was very powerful and Reneau wanted to establish from the onset that he was the one in control.

An interesting twist to the story is that Coach Barmore decided to un-retire after I took the job at Baylor. In effect, Dan Reneau cut off his nose to spite his face and they had no where else to turn. Coach Barmore loved the Lady Techster program, so he bailed Reneau out and stayed a couple more years to keep the program going. I'm forever grateful to Coach Barmore for stepping aside and giving me the opportunity. I know he did it because he didn't want me to leave and he wanted me to be the next head coach at Tech. I've heard that Dan Reneau has said that he has never regretted his decision to not give me the five-year contract. The regret I have is all the negative publicity that came out of it because I gave my heart and soul to Louisiana Tech. Isn't it amazing, since I left Dan Reneau has given five-year contracts to newly hired coaches.

"It was an absolute shame that we couldn't keep Kim," Barmore said. "Who suffered? Louisiana Tech suffered. The fans suffered. It hurt our program. She is made up a lot like I am. Louisiana Tech was all she knew and it's all she wanted."

Coach Barmore and I never got to coach against each other after I left for Baylor in 2000. "That would have been something," he says today. "When we both made the NCAA Tournament that first year I thought maybe the NCAA would put us together in the same region." However, Baylor was put in the West Regional and Louisiana Tech was slotted in the East."

In 2002, the two schools were in the same regional, but Baylor, the No. 2 seed after a 26–5 regular season, was upset at home by Drake in the second round while No. 12 seed California-Santa Barbara won over Louisiana Tech, a No. 5 seed after a 25–4 season, in the first round.

The current Louisiana Tech coach, Chris Long, was hired by Dan Reneau in 2005. He was an assistant coach at Louisiana Tech for the previous six seasons. In a press release announcing his hiring it was noted that "Having been courted for several Division I head coaching jobs around the country during that time, the Vicksburg, Mississippi native showed his loyalty by staying at Louisiana Tech." Reneau went on to say, "In my opinion,

Chris Long is the perfect fit for this program. He is very popular with our fans and his own players and possesses great coaching talents. He obviously is the man for this job."

It's tough to sustain a quality program. It's a different era now. You have more schools putting more money into their programs and building nicer facilities. At a mid-major school like Louisiana Tech it's tough to maintain the level of excellence year after year. Coach Barmore always said, "When you lose it, you'll never get it back." They lost him. I'm not sure they'll ever get it back.

A few months later I was inducted into the Women's Basketball Hall of Fame in Knoxville, Tennessee. A busload of Louisiana Tech fans and friends traveled there to share in that special moment with me. All the years at Louisiana Tech, all the battles with Coach Barmore, and all the hard work to keep the Lady Techster program at the top made me into what I am today, both as a coach and as a woman.

5

Family Matters

On June 6, 1987, I was married in the Trinity United Methodist Church in Ruston. The church sits atop a small hill overlooking the interstate. It was an evening ceremony and I walked down the aisle to the traditional "Bridal March." My sister, Tammy, who had recently married my brother-in-law, James (Jimbo) Zievert, was my matron of honor. I had eight bridesmaids, including Jennifer White and the two Tuten daughters, Maribel and Maradith. The local newspaper in Hammond printed a picture of me in my wedding dress with a caption reading, "Mrs. Randy Robertson . . . She was Kim Mulkey." I became Kim Mulkey-Robertson that day.

Randy and I met during my sophomore year at Louisiana Tech. He was eight years older than I was, but as Mary Belle Tuten always said, if I ever did get serious in a relationship it would have to be with an older man because I'd been around adults my whole life. I credit Mary Belle for playing the role of matchmaker in our relationship. She would repeatedly mention that she met this cute guy on campus, a former Tech football player who worked in the university's athletic promotions department. She never let up.

The first time I met Randy was at a banquet for the basketball team. I can remember thinking that he was dressed so neatly! Can you imagine that? From head to toe, I thought he looked sharp. Great shoes, the whole thing. I can also remember how he was always making eye contact with me. Every time I looked his way, I'd notice that he had his eyes on me.

One of our very first "dates," if you can call it that, was at the Tuten's house. The university was in the middle of winter break, but I was still on campus because the basketball season was in full swing. Mary Belle invited me over to lunch one day after practice. Randy was invited, too. This was Mary Belle at her matchmaking best. Well, it turned out that it snowed that day and Randy was afraid I might have trouble with the road conditions. (We don't get a lot of snow in Louisiana so I wasn't accustomed to driving in that kind of weather, but I certainly was going to try.) Randy sweetly followed right behind in his car, making sure I got there safely.

Randy's family was from the State of Washington, but his father was in the plywood business and moved around quite a bit. Randy likes to say that he was a gypsy because he never lived in one place for very long. His first two years of high school he was a quarterback and then switched to a wide receiver when he moved from Byrd High School in Shreveport to Broadmoor High School in Baton Rouge. He was recruited by Louisiana Tech as a quarterback. In fact, Randy played quarterback at Louisiana Tech from 1972–77 and graduated in 1977. He was part of the Division II national championship team in 1973.

We were alike in so many ways, but also so very different. One thing we definitely had in common was our love of sports. Where we tended to differ was in socializing. In college my friends were my teammates and if I wasn't with them I was over at the Tutens. I entertained myself—not that it took much. The things that made me happy then, and now, were rooted in home and family. As I've said, I'm content with the simple things in life—a ballgame on television or a good book or magazine. I've only attended two concerts in my life: Kiss and Air Supply. If you want to hang out with me, you better be prepared to be bored. During my four years of college, I probably only went to two fraternity parties. To this day, I have never had a drop of alcohol, although I'm not opposed to it. I've simply never been tempted by it. I am a proud person and I never want to get intoxicated and lose control. Truly, what you don't know you don't miss.

Randy was much more extroverted. This is probably why he works in the promotions business. He enjoys people. He's a communicator. He can sit down and start a conversation with anyone and people love to talk to him. They enjoy him as much as he does them.

In those days, Randy often traveled with the Lady Techsters in his role as promotions director with the athletic department. We found ways to eat at the same table or grab a few precious moments, but we were careful to avoid any suspicion. My life then was focused on two things: academics and basketball. Our idea of a "date" was grabbing a bite to eat or watching a ballgame on television.

We dated for five years, but it was far from a typical relationship. There were long periods of time when we didn't see each other, mainly in the summers when I was playing in exotic locales for USA Basketball. He was able, however, to come to Los Angeles in 1984 and enjoy the Olympic experience with my parents.

We had some fun times during those early years. I can remember once hiring a woman to flash Randy at his home on Halloween. She went to the front door, rang the doorbell, and when he answered she opened her coat and said, "Trick or treat!"

Randy surprised me one special day, too. He gave me a jack-in-the-box. After winding it up, the jack popped out with a small black box and a note that said, "Will you marry me?" I was totally surprised, because although we had dated for so long, neither one of us was in a rush to get married.

At the time my father and I had a strained relationship. He and my mother divorced two years earlier and I was still upset and angry about the split. His unfaithfulness to my mother devastated our entire family. I would never have imagined my dad doing what he did—ever.

I thought I could deal with it. It was a hurtful time for my mother, my sister, and me. I wish I could say that because I was older it didn't hurt as much or that I was better equipped to cope with it, but no matter my age, it was very difficult to get through. I worshipped my father. With all of my sports activities I filled the role of a son for him. He was so proud of me and I was so proud that he was my dad.

Randy and I started making wedding plans six months before the big day. By this time my father had remarried and I didn't even know the woman. One day they visited my duplex and it was not a pretty scene. To this day, I truly don't know why they came. I guess he wanted me to meet her or maybe she wanted to meet me. He may have been hoping that he might get my approval somehow. I vented, telling him that I didn't like the way he had handled things. He had gotten a quickie divorce in Haiti, and in my eyes, he wasn't legally married to her. He was showing no respect to my mother, my sister, or me. At that point, I really didn't care what he thought or what I said. I distinctly remember asking his new wife, "Do you really think that after what he's done to my mother he's not going to do the same thing to you?" I was crying and saying ugly things. It remains the one and only time I have ever met the woman. My father tried to reason with me, but we were two people with two very different versions of right and wrong. Even after that painful episode I told myself, "It's going to be fine." I know my father. Although our relationship had become strained, I was hopeful that things would work themselves out.

As our wedding plans progressed my father sent in his order for his tuxedo, along with money to pay for it. However, things changed for the worse. One day on the telephone I made it clear to him that after he walked me down the aisle, he would be sitting in the second pew behind my mother. His new wife would not be sitting in the first few rows. This made him extremely angry. I told him, "I'm sorry, daddy, but you are not going to use my wedding to tell the congregation and all the family that I have accepted what you've done. I've only met the woman once in my life." I did offer him a compromise. He could sit in his assigned second pew seat and his new wife could sit directly behind him in a pew that was not "within the ribbons." He continued to insist that she sit with him. There was no way that was going to happen and I said, "This is my day. I can do whatever I want to do. This is the way it's going to be."

In the end, my father did not attend my wedding. I know friends of our family tried to get him to change his mind, but he wouldn't budge—and neither would I. Randy even sent him a registered letter before the wedding asking him to reconsider but there was no reply. I walked down the aisle by myself. It was no big deal. I could have had an uncle, a cousin, or even a friend accompany me, but I decided to do it myself. I thought,

"You're 25 years old, you're independent, and this is your day."

My father and I have not had a conversation since that day. It's sad, but I warned him back then that he had better make sure he understood the consequences of what he was doing. It was the last obligation he had to me as a daughter and I made it clear to him that my wishes needed to come before his that day. I was not going to back down. He put himself first when he chose to break up our family and I had no control over his decision, but he wasn't going to put himself first on my day.

I'm sure he regrets what he's done. He has sent me notes since then, but I have never opened them. I simply mark them "return to sender." You just don't do that to your daughter. No second or third wife is more important than your daughter is on her wedding day. That day is hers. He should have respected my wishes.

None of this takes away from the fact that, while I was growing up and going to college, he was a wonderful father. He came to all of my games. He provided for my sister and me, and we had a great father–daughter relationship.

I am very close with my mother to this day. She has an absolutely forgiving personality. Even before my wedding, she had already put the divorce behind her. My mother didn't get nearly as angry as I did about her divorce. She has always wanted me to have a relationship with my father, and to this day, I am certain she wants me to reach out to him. While I love my mother dearly, our personalities are very different. In the first few years after my wedding, my mother and sister would bring up my father in conversation. After awhile I made it clear that the reconciliation they hoped for was not going to happen and there was no use bringing up the topic. We don't discuss my father anymore.

My mother moved from the family home in Tickfaw to a house a short distance away in Hammond. At that time my mother was working as an office manager in a doctor's office where she continued to work for more than 30 years. She is now retired and her mother, Nora Wiley, whom we all lovingly call "Nanny," lives with her.

My sister lives with her family in Vinton, which is located in southwest Louisiana. She has two children. Her daughter, Bailey, is an excellent softball player and a two-time state high school champion javelin thrower. Her other child, Clem, is very much his mother's son. He loves showing his prized animals at 4-H shows. Tammy and I are not close in the sense that we talk on the phone every week or even every month. But we are sisters and if she needs something from me, she knows that I am there for her. She has, above all, the softest, softest heart.

6

Family Life

Randy and I waited more than four years after we were married to have our first child, Makenzie Marie. She was born on September 16, 1991. Her dad named her, but I can't explain why he chose the name. All I know is that he was adamant that her name not be spelled with a "c" because he didn't want anyone calling her "Mack." For the most part it has worked.

Three years almost to the day my little man, Kramer, arrived. He was born on September 20, 1994. I named our son. When I was in college I read an article in a *Fellowship of Christian Athletes* magazine about one of Steve Largent's children who was born with spina bifida. Largent is a former NFL receiver who is now in politics. His son's name was Kramer. I thought it was an unusual name and a great story. I said to myself, if I ever have a son, I will name him Kramer.

My mother loves to tease me about my children being New Year's Eve babies. She did the math and figured out that they were both conceived on New Year's Eve. There was a time when my mom would call at midnight every New Year's to tease us—"Hey, what are you guys doing?" Well, I think you get the idea.

Both of my children were brought into this world with a crowd of spectators. They were born at Lincoln General Hospital in Ruston, Louisiana. The doctor said, "I don't have a problem with all these people in here if the administration doesn't." Allen Tuten was the hospital administrator and he was like a second father to me, which was especially meaningful given my estrangement from my own father. I remember Nell Fortner, who was an assistant coach with me, standing there in amazement. She couldn't believe that I was delivering a baby with my glasses on and my mouth running, talking to everyone there. She swore I made it look easy. I had epidurals with both deliveries, so it really wasn't all that painful or ugly. They were very uncomplicated deliveries, even though labor was induced both times because my blood pressure had risen dangerously high.

When I was seven months pregnant with Makenzie we hired Annie Talbert to help out with her. One afternoon I was outside cutting the grass on our rider mower—something I love to do—and I stopped to talk to our next-door neighbor. She inquired about what I was going to do when the baby came. Was I going to keep coaching? I told her I was, but we still hadn't hired someone to help with the new baby. She told me about a woman, now retired, that helped with her children. "You won't be lucky enough to have what I had," she told me. But she volunteered to call her just in case the woman had an interest in helping us out.

Needless to say, Annie, who is my mother's age, was interested. She was a godsend. She lived 20 minutes away, and when needed, she would spend the night at our house. She even traveled with me on recruiting trips. She was and still is a big part of our lives and our family. Annie started when Makenzie was two weeks old and helped us out until we moved to Waco nine years later. I had more trouble leaving her than I did leaving Louisiana Tech. My children absolutely adore her and affectionately call her, "my Annie."

Being a mother and a coach is not easy, but regardless of how tough it can get, I love every minute of it. I vividly remember coaching against Tennessee when I was three months pregnant with Makenzie. It was very traumatic for me to even be pregnant. My body was going through all these changes and the enormity of the commitment I was making overwhelmed me. Nothing anybody told me made me feel better until I talked to someone in a similar line of work with the same goals and career aspirations.

Pat Summitt visited with me at great length before one of her teams games against Louisiana Tech. Only after that meeting did I feel a lot better. I could ask her about things that were bothering me about my pregnancy. She had gone through the same kinds of things with her pregnancy. My conversation with Pat about children and pregnancy was just as important to me, if not more important, than when we won an Olympic gold medal together. "I wanted her to know that everything she was going through was going to be worth it in the end," Summitt says. "You have to have some kind of balance in your life between the personal and the professional. My son was always involved in my career. He was around my teams. He was at Picture Day. I took him with me on the road. It can be a great life for kids and it's very gratifying to be able to share that with your family. I know Kim feels the same way now. But back then, she didn't know."

I breast-fed both of my children because it was the healthy thing to do for them. I did it for six months with Makenzie and four months with Kramer, and looking back, I'd do the same thing again. I would have to breast-feed on a regular schedule before or after our practices and games. Sometimes that got a little awkward. During the 1991–92 season, a couple of months after Makenzie was born, our team played in a tournament in Hawaii. I had to pump breast milk so I could leave it at home for her and continue pumping while I was in Hawaii. Talk about being committed! Nevertheless, it was the kind of dedication that was important to me. I wanted to put just as much of myself into being a good mother as I did into being a good coach. Most importantly, I always wanted to make sure that we raised our own kids. Even if we had to hire help, we didn't want someone else raising them.

When I went on recruiting trips, I would take the babies with me. I took Makenzie on a trip when she was just two weeks old. Whatever I had to do to make it work—I did it. If I had to pull over on the side of the road to breast-feed, I would do it. The children continued to go with me as they grew older and I can even remember Makenzie making suggestions to me about which players she liked the most. I think Kramer's best memories of me on the recruiting trail are sitting in the stands taking notes. They have seen a lot of high school basketball games as children. They have seen an even greater number of college games. As a result, they're not afraid to tell me what they think!

After games nowadays, they ride home with me in the car and it's rare when they don't ask me something about the game or say something that might crack me up. I remember after playing a game against Iowa State once Kramer asked, "Mom, did you have to say 'damn' out there?" I'm thinking to myself, "OK, how do I wiggle out of this one?" Finally, I dug up one of those handy parenting adages and said, "Don't do as I do, do as I say." For good measure I added, "And I better never hear you say a cuss word!" His look told me that the answer didn't satisfy him. They question why I don't play a particular girl more or why I put someone in at a certain time. They watch and pay attention to what is going on during the game.

It may be hard for someone on the outside to understand their depth and knowledge of the game, but my children see what the average child does not see because this is what they've known and grown up with all their lives. I'm proud of their insight into the game. Nevertheless, sometimes, especially after a loss, I have to tell them, "I don't feel like explaining game strategy. I don't want to talk about it." Three or four days will pass and Kramer will usually bring it up again.

In my profession they love you when you win and they fire you when you lose. I taught my children at a young age that they may hear ugly things said about their mother, the coach. I joke with them and remind them not to tell anyone who their mother really is.

When I came to Baylor, one of the first things I told the administration was that my family was very important to me. I was going to do my job, but they needed to know that if there was an emergency or if something arose with a member of my family the decision was already made. My family would come first. They were completely fine with that.

I try to go to as many of my children's sporting events as my time and schedule allow. I love attending their practices as well as their games. As my children get older, I know there will be games I won't be able to see, but I try to be as active and hands-on as I can be. I can always coach, but my children are only going to be with me until high school is over and then they will move on to college and their adult lives. I don't want to wake up one day wondering where all the years went. What I want is an abundant collection of great moments and memories that we've shared. I want them to remember that I had a career that was pressure-packed, stressful, and sometimes took me away at Thanksgiving and Christmas, but I made sure they were never neglected. It's often a balancing act making every effort to do my job and leaving to attend their functions.

When I am not attending their games, I love to work in the yard, whether it's mowing the lawn or working in my flower beds. It's relaxing and therapeutic to me. It's not that I am a loner or an introvert. It's just that with all the arenas that I've been in over the years and all the public attention and scrutiny that comes with my job, I really want my free time to be my personal time.

I love to listen to music, although anyone who knows me will tell you that I can't carry a tune to save my life. One of my favorite recordings is the soundtrack to the *The Graduate* by Simon and Garfunkel. I am also a fan of gospel and country music. In college, Ronnie Millsap was my favorite entertainer. As I started coaching and making recruiting trips, I found myself gravitating more toward country music. I would be driving at night, usually alone, and I'd turn on the radio and listen to the words. When you're young you listen to the beat. When you get older you listen to the lyrics, which remind you of things that happened in your own life.

I like all music except some of the modern stuff. I love good, old-fashioned church hymns—"Amazing Grace," "How Great Thou Art," and "The Old Rugged Cross." I have told my children that I would like a collection of church hymns played at my memorial service. Those are some of the hymns I learned while I was growing up and attending church in Natalbany.

We try to be regular churchgoers but sometimes the kids' sports tournaments and activities keep us busy on Sundays. The children and I say prayers together every night. It's a part of our daily lives. Every night I say my own prayers. I don't read the Bible as much as I should nor do I tote one around with me everywhere I go. I know my weaknesses. When I go to bed I pray for forgiveness and thank the Lord for all my blessings.

Too many people get caught up in judging you by what religion you are. I'm not into that. It's not me. I'm going to respect you for who you are regardless of your denomination. As I've grown older I believe each of us should be true to ourselves. It's more important to just do the right thing as a person.

My children are as involved with my teams as they can be. When they can go on trips with me they do. They traveled with me during our run to the championship, and to this day, they list Seattle as their favorite place to have gone with the Lady Bears. My son Kramer often reminds me that they liked Indianapolis and the really big hotel suite, too. Indianapolis, after all, was the city where we won the NCAA championship.

My children have developed an excellent work ethic. I feel very blessed that we instilled it in them at an early age. They are both respectful and excellent students. I never have to hound them about their homework. They come home, they go to their practices, they do their schoolwork, and I never have to worry. I hope it always remains that way. It would be absolute misery for me to come home and have to fight with them over their schoolwork.

People who know Makenzie say she is very much her mother's daughter. Makenzie is a perfectionist like me. She wakes up early, spends a full day at school, travels with her team to away games, gets home late, grabs some supper somewhere along the way, and stays up late doing homework, sometimes into the wee hours of the morning. She studies and works until she feels like everything is done just right.

It makes me very proud to see how self-disciplined she is. When we moved to Waco her fourth-grade teacher called home one day and was planning to plead with me to take it easy on my daughter; I was putting way too much pressure on her to succeed in and out of the classroom. I told the teacher, Mary Lou Glaesmann, who has since become one of my best friends, that I was not putting any pressure on Makenzie; it all came from within her. She was born that way. I know my mother would have said the same thing had a teacher called her to say those very same things about me.

It is somewhat of a surprise to me to see how athletic my children are. They benefit from athletic genes, but they also deserve credit for working hard. Makenzie plays several sports, but her favorite is basketball. She wears her hair in a ponytail or occasionally mom's famous pigtails. She plays shooting guard and some point guard. Both her basketball team and her softball team have had a lot of success over the last few years. She played on two Little League softball World Series championship teams. We traveled as a family to Beaverton, Oregon to watch them win it all. She plays in the same AAU basketball organization that I played in when I was in high school. The AAU coach, Charlie Domino, called to congratulate me on winning the National Championship and wondered if Makenzie might be interested in playing for the team. I thought it would be a great experience for her, but I also knew she was so committed to softball in the summer that it would be difficult time-wise for her to play both sports. However, the coach worked it out so that she could do both. She flies to New Orleans on weekends during the summer to practice with the basketball team when she is not playing softball. My mother picks her up at the airport and they stay with one of my mom's friends, who lives in nearby Kenner. During the summer of 2006, Makenzie ended up playing in her first national AAU tournament. It was her first exposure playing against the top players across the country. If she keeps playing well I don't foresee any recruiting battle for her. She'll play for me.

Makenzie has many academic interests. Most notably, she is an unbelievable writer. Her writing skills amaze me. Who knows maybe she will be a sports writer one day!

Personality wise Makenzie is very sensitive and her moral compass is pointed in the right direction. She inherited her grey eyes from me—the same color as my paternal grandmother. The eyes are the focal point of her face. When you speak to her you are automatically drawn to those eyes. It is such a blessing to see the young lady that she is becoming.

Kramer, on the other hand, makes good grades but doesn't stress himself in the process. He is active in sports. He plays quarterback just like his dad and he plays shortstop, pitcher, and catcher in baseball. In basketball, like his mom, he plays point guard.

Kramer is always out on the court before Baylor home games shooting three pointers. He is a crowd pleaser. When he first started his pre-game show he was only six years old and it took everything in his little body to throw that basketball from the three-point line far enough to reach the basket. The fans would hold their breath as they watched him hurl that basketball, seeing it sit on the rim teetering back and forth and uttering a collective sigh of relief when it fell through the basket.

During my second year at Baylor, I attended the annual Chamber of Commerce Tip-Off Luncheon. There is always a huge gathering at this luncheon, and in the past, we've had guest speakers like Bob Knight and Van Chancellor. The four college coaches from the area speak at this event—the men's and women's coaches from Baylor and the men's and women's coaches from McLennan Community College. Kevin Gill, the McLennan's men's coach, spoke about his summer basketball camp and this "little kid that was in his camp." He talked about how this little fellow could handle the ball, run the drills, shoot, pass—do it all. He watched him every day and finally on the last day of camp he walked up to an unsuspecting Kramer, rubbed his head and complimented him on his skills. Gill said he told him, "You're really good, kid. Your daddy must be quite a basketball player." Gill said Kramer looked up at him, shook his head, and said, "No sir, my momma is Kim Mulkey!"

Kramer has these big, soulful brown eyes that just melt my heart. He acts as if he has a tougher core than Makenzie, but deep inside he has always been my worrier. When he was younger he was always concerned about things and would ask me questions such as, "Mom, is it a Ten Commandment to . . .?" or "Mom, is it against the law to . . .?" Kramer's always wondering and thinking about things, often things that seem beyond his years. Because he has an older sibling, he is much more mature than friends his own age.

Kramer also has a great sense of humor. He tells his friends that his mom yells just as much at home as she does during a basketball game, but then adds that she's really a lot nicer than she seems. Once he's comfortable with you he likes to joke around and cut up. He's very quick-witted. We tease Kramer about his self-confidence. As he will quickly let you know, "It's all about him."

Just like other parents, I love my children uncondi-tionally. While I am very proud of them, I also realize how very fortunate I am to be their mother.

7

Building a Program

｡ᐧᐞ

Baylor University is the oldest, continually operating institution of higher learning in the State of Texas. It is also the
world's largest Baptist university with an enrollment of
nearly 14,000 and is the only private school in the Big 12
Conference.

The Baylor campus represents a blend of old and new with
Victorian and Georgian architecture as well as more
modern designs for dormitories and classrooms. The university might be the only one in the country to have two
live black bears on campus. They are the school's mascots
and they live in the center of campus in a specially
designed habitat known as the Bear Pit. A local service
organization cares for the bears, who make appearances at

football games and other school events. The main administration building, Pat Neff Hall, has a dome that lights up green every time a Baylor athletic team wins a game.

Baylor is located in the city of Waco, Texas, which has a population of around 115,000. Among the famous Waco-ites are actor Steve Martin, actress Jennifer Love Hewitt, 2006 NFL Most Valuable Player LaDanian Tomlinson of the San Diego Chargers, and noted baby doctor T. Berry Brazelton. Waco is also the home of the soft drink Dr Pepper, created in 1885.

The city is sometimes called "the Heart of Texas" because of its location in the central part of the massive state. It is home to the 22-story ALICO building which was the tallest building west of the Mississippi when it was constructed in 1910. Thirty-five parks, including one measuring 416 acres, dot the city, which has an average mean temperature of 67 degrees. There is also Lake Waco (7,000 acres), which is one of the prime recreation areas in Waco. Kim Mulkey can sometimes be seen jet skiing on the lake in the summertime.

Waco is unfairly linked to one of the more horrifying incidents in recent American history—the 1993 siege of the Branch Davidian compound. The 51-day standoff ended with the loss of more than 80 lives in a fiery confrontation. The Branch Davidian compound was not located in Waco but on the outskirts, some 10 miles to the east. However, the city is now inextricably linked to the incident, so much so that the respected PBS show *Frontline* aired a soup-to-nuts broadcast of the incident in 1995 and titled it, "Waco: The Inside Story."

In 2000, Athletic Director Tom Stanton had an opening for the head women's basketball coach when Coach Sonja Hogg—the same woman who had recruited Kim Mulkey to play and coach at Louisiana Tech—announced in February that it was time for her to retire. Hogg had coached six years at Baylor, and as she was walking out the door, she mentioned to Stanton the person who she felt would be a perfect successor: Kim Mulkey.

Stanton was hoping simply to build something which in five to seven years would be viewed as a regular Top 20 program, a place that marquee high school players would consider choosing along with the likes of Connecticut, Tennessee, and the other national powers.

Stanton had three names on his wish list for the new women's head coach at Baylor: Clemson coach Jim Davis, Arkansas coach Gary Blair, and Mulkey, the associate head coach at Louisiana Tech. He felt that it would be difficult to pry Mulkey away from Louisiana Tech, but he also saw in her the qualities he wanted in all of his coaches.

"She was the kind of hire that the university needed to make in order to break a string of 25 years in which Baylor was just a training ground. She had the leadership skills that I wanted. She had integrity. She was intelligent and accomplished. From a leadership standpoint alone, you could envision her one day running a Fortune 500 company."

Indeed, the former football coach at Baylor, Grant Teaff, has said that he thinks Mulkey would have had no problem coaching men's football for those very reasons. "She's just the embodiment of everything that you'd ever want in a coach," Teaff said. "I told her a couple of years ago: 'Kim, you can coach my sport. There's no doubt in my mind. That's what I live with every day, and you can coach it."

It was only natural to have second thoughts after I took the Baylor job. Having never lived anywhere else but Louisiana—and never expecting to—it was a huge change.

Before that first season started I visited the Branch Davidian compound outside Waco. Everyone had watched what happened there and I was very curious and wanted to see it. It turned out that my next-door neighbor when I finally moved to a house outside of the city was Burton Lawless, the former lineman for the University of Florida and the Dallas Cowboys.

Burton and I have become close friends over the years and every time my mother is in town he makes sure to stop by and say hello to "his girlfriend." I call him "a fat old lineman" and he has season tickets to all the Lady Bears' basketball games. When we played Florida a few years back Burton and his son, Denver, flew with us to be at the game. (I hope he was rooting for the Lady Bears!)

Burton drove me and my mother out to see the Branch Davidian compound site. I was in the back seat and as we approached the compound a woman who was handing out informational pamphlets stopped the car. Burton told her that he was just taking a couple of friends to see the compound. The woman looked in the car and recognized me immediately saying, "I've seen you on television. Welcome to Waco, Coach."

I'm glad I went to see where it all happened, but it was an eerie feeling. I recognized parts of it from television. But the thing I'll remember most about the drive was seeing a cow give birth on the side of the road and my mother being worried there was no veterinarian around to help.

One thing I quickly realized is that the Branch Davidian compound is not in Waco; it's probably 10 minutes outside of the city. Waco is the closest city, though, so it gets associated with the compound. President Bush's ranch in Crawford is actually closer to Waco than the Branch Davidian Compound.

For the first two or three months I was still an emotional wreck because of everything that took place at Louisiana Tech. I would lie in bed at night and think, "Did I make the right decision?" I'd rehash and rethink all the things that happened. I lived in an apartment with my assistant, Jennifer Roberts, while Randy and the kids stayed in Ruston to finish out the school year. Thankfully, we quickly became engrossed in our work and I no longer had time to think like that anymore. I had a job to do and it was time to move forward.

At the press conference that introduced me to the Baylor community all of my feelings bubbled up inside of me. As I stood at the podium my voice cracked and tears welled in my eyes. I didn't even realize it until someone told me later. My husband said he was so nervous because he thought I might just stand up there and say, "I can't do this. I'm going back to Louisiana Tech."

From the beginning I knew it was important for me to hire the right staff. I wanted people loyal to me. I wanted them to be ambitious and have their own goals and I didn't want people who would be with me for a year and move on. I needed to surround myself with people who would do a topnotch job and be persistent. They had to want a challenge because building this program was definitely going to be one. I decided to run the team like a CEO. I was going to do the coaching—I didn't need anyone else to do that. I was going to make the decisions—I am not a very patient person and I was especially hungry that first season. All I needed was a good team supporting me.

My first need was to hire a business-oriented person, so I asked Johnny Derrick to come with me from Louisiana. In his 24 years with CGU Insurance in Ruston he had risen through the ranks of the company. I had befriended Johnny when he was a fan at Louisiana Tech. He is a man who knows his stuff without having a basketball coaching background. I enjoy his company and respect his administrative skills. I knew he could deal with the money, handle the scheduling, and do all the necessary paperwork required by the conference and the NCAA. He is efficient and meticulous. When we go on trips Johnny turns in the reports on time, to the dime. I didn't want to be burdened with the pressure of doing it. I thought Johnny would be the best person to answer the administrators' questions about money, budgets, and scheduling. Boy, was I right. I always believe that when coaches are fired it isn't just because of wins and losses. It can be for other reasons including going over budget. Johnny also has a calming personality and he makes outstanding suggestions on tough decisions that need to be made on the floor. He is patient and caring, and make no mistake about it, he knows the game of basketball as well as anyone I've ever been around.

My next hire was Jennifer Roberts. She was young. She was around the Louisiana Tech program as a manager and a graduate assistant. She had also helped her father start an AAU program in Shreveport, Louisiana. So I knew she could relate to the new era of players and talk their talk. She was personable and pleasant and she could recruit. I liked her. Jennifer is the most loyal person I have ever met. She handles our players wonderfully and is attentive to their needs. Each year she brings better and better players to our program.

I needed someone with contacts in the recruiting world in the state of Texas, as well as experience in the coaching profession, for my third hire. That's where Bill Brock entered the picture. I knew Bill through recruiting and I found him to always be very professional. He was the head coach at Grayson County College for the last 13 years and in one of those seasons his team went 36–1, finishing third in the National Junior College Athletic Association Tournament. I also liked the fact that so many of Bill's players—more than 60—had received scholarships and continued to play basketball after they left Grayson. He strongly emphasized academics, which is one of the hallmarks at Baylor.

Those first three coaching hires—Bill, Jennifer, and Johnny—were unconventional ones. Only Bill had traditional basketball experience. Even though I knew Jennifer and Johnny had no coaching experience, I knew what I needed them to do and that they'd be the perfect fit.

Once the assistants were on board, I had to sit in that chair and say, "Okay, big girl, all the decisions now rest on your shoulders." I don't live in an unrealistic world. I knew we couldn't recruit against the so-called powers-that-be for the best players. We needed to focus on high school and junior college players who could help us compete and improve. We were at the bottom of the Big 12 Conference. The goal was not to win the Big 12—that was unrealistic. Instead the goal was to see how many rungs up the ladder we could move. We needed to find players who were better than what we inherited, players who might help us move up into the middle of the pack.

We beat the bushes and along the way kept our eye out for the sleeper who might have been overlooked by other schools. This was how we started the building process.

One advantage is that Baylor sells itself academically. Its academic reputation is outstanding. In the minds of many people it is the so-called "academic institution" of the Big 12, much like Stanford is in the PAC 10 and Vanderbilt is in the Southeastern Conference. Therefore, we only had to build athletically. We had the finances, the facilities, and the support of the administration. All that was left was for us to roll up our sleeves and get to work.

One of my first decisions was to bring in junior college recruits to start the building process, one of whom was Sheila Lambert. She had played for Bill Brock at Grayson County College. A lot of people still think it was a package deal but that couldn't be further from the truth. It's true that many times coaches hire other coaches simply to get a certain player and there's nothing wrong with that, but that's not what happened in this case.

When I first talked to Sheila I told her that we weren't good enough for her yet. I told her that she should go to Louisiana Tech. I still felt loyal to the school in spite of everything that had happened. Their program was much further along than Baylor's. However, she decided against Tech because of a conflict she had with one of the assistants who had just been hired there. I remember Brock asking, "Are you sure you don't want Sheila Lambert? Because she's not going to Louisiana Tech." I replied, "Whoa! We will definitely recruit her if she isn't going to go to Tech."

I know Sheila visited several schools, but there are a lot of major programs that don't recruit junior college kids. Maybe they think they're flawed because they didn't go straight from high school to a four-year college team; I don't really know. Some coaches have the mentality that they are only going to recruit high school kids and that's fine.

Sheila could have played anywhere in the country, she was that good. We were very fortunate to have her come to Baylor. She was a tremendous influence on the basketball team and from the moment she arrived on campus her teammates knew how good she was. She was the first Kodak All-American I coached at Baylor.

After her senior year she was drafted by the WNBA and left Baylor. However, as great a player as Sheila was in helping us jump start our program, I told her we would not retire her number until she got her degree from Baylor. I bugged her persistently about coming back and finishing her courses and in May of 2006 she finally earned her degree. When we retired her jersey on January 3, 2007, there was no one more proud of her than me.

There were two other junior college players we had that first year, Carla Mathisen and Brooke McCormack. They were also from Grayson and both natives of Australia. Carla didn't stick around for long. She decided to return to Australia before we even had our first practice. While the timing could have been better, I did appreciate Carla's honesty in the matter. She was 23 years old and it was going to take her three years to get a degree in psychology from Baylor. She could get the same degree in Australia in 18 months. I think she wanted to get on with her life and it wasn't in her heart to be at Baylor. She probably would have been miserable and life is too short for that.

Brooke played in all 30 games the first season, most of the time as the first player off the bench. She proved to be an even more important signing when one of my senior centers, Michelle Neely, went down midseason with a torn ACL. Brooke ended up playing for us for two years.

Building confidence in the players you've inherited is where you start as a new coach. You then try to bring in some good players—better players hopefully—that will help you compete in the Big 12 Conference. It is a very tough conference to build in because the teams are so good. There is terrific competition and exposure. For this same reason it can also be a very easy conference to recruit to. We let our early recruits know they would have a good chance to play immediately.

When I took the job at Baylor I felt that I had to be hard-nosed with the players in order to change the atmosphere of losing. I was 38 years old. It was my first head coaching job and I told myself, "You can't be a softie." It was a transition period for Baylor and changes needed to be made. The team had only won seven games the year before I got there but there are a lot of reasons why teams lose. It can be chemistry. It can be a lack of talent. Whatever the reason it was my job to change it.

My coaching style may not motivate every player. I tell the kids up front that I coach off of emotion. That's the way I played and it's the only way I know. I'm brutally honest with them. I want them to play hard. I demand it of them and I demand it of myself. All of my players know before they come to Baylor that I am very demanding. I tell them what to expect and how I coach before they ever set foot on campus.

One of the first players to came see me was Danielle Crockrom. She had been the leading scorer, but had quit the team the year before. She wanted to come back and play for me. I talked to her. I challenged her. I told her, "I'm not sure you can handle my style and I don't want you to come back if you can't handle it and you're going to quit again. I don't want quitters." I told her to think about it. In a way I was trying to scare her away. I just didn't want her to come back again if she was going to turn around and quit when I challenged her.

I think it's important to set the right tone from the start. Danielle decided she could handle my style and ended up coming back and being a great player for us. She blossomed and was even drafted by the WNBA. Many times Danielle has publicly given me credit for motivating her and turning her career around. That sounds and makes me feel good, but Danielle is the one who did it. All she needed was someone to challenge, motivate, and believe in her. She made All-Conference and graduated from Baylor, ending her college career on a positive note. That is something you want for all your players.

Then there was Brittany Bruns who was going to be a senior and who had played for three years, including one year for me. I was going to choose her to be one of our captains her senior year. At the end of the season she came into my office and told me that no matter how hard she worked or how much she improved she saw that we were bringing in better players and she didn't think she'd ever get the chance to play. She also said she was tired of playing basketball and started to cry. Brittany told me she was going to stay at Baylor and finish her degree, but she felt horrible abandoning her basketball scholarship and having to ask her parents to pay for the last year of school just because she was burnt-out. She felt selfish asking such a thing of them.

Because I had not used all of my allotted 15 scholarships I still had one available for her. I didn't want her parents to have to pay for her last year at Baylor, so I told her she could come to my office once a week and check in with the secretary to see what work needed to be done in exchange for keeping her scholarship. I thought it was a great way of putting that 15th scholarship to use. She came in and pro-moted the team, helping with some marketing, doing some public speaking, and trying to get younger people to come see the Lady Bears play.

"Coach really took care of me when she didn't have to," Bruns says. "She could have used that last scholarship to improve the team and bring in a player, but she didn't. I don't know why she did it, but I am forever indebted to that woman. I didn't have to worry after that. I was so upset because I didn't want my parents to have to pay tuition; it's really expensive at Baylor. I almost felt like a brat because I was tired of playing and it had absolutely nothing to do with her. And I told her that. She just said, 'Brittany, I'll look into this' and gave me a big hug. I knew there was a scholarship open, but I had no idea she would do what she did. Everything fell into place and it was like there was this big weight lifted off my shoulders. I owe that woman, big time."

I have a certain allegiance to every one of my players but for different reasons. Some leave Baylor and I never hear from them again, maybe they just didn't like me. Some leave and call or email often, expressing their gratitude for their time at Baylor and for what we tried to do for them. That's life. What makes me the most proud is that like me or not, the kids who stayed with the program, left with a degree in their hand. There has never been a player who started her college career playing for me, remained at Baylor, and did not leave school with a degree. These kids come from all walks of life. Some got straight A's. Some struggled to get through. It didn't matter to me; I made sure they made it. I'm proud of those who were role players and just as proud of those who were All-Americans. I'm proud of the ones that went on to play professionally or to coach, and those who got jobs that had nothing to do with basketball. They're all Baylor graduates, I'm most proud of that.

You don't have to be a star player to be considered a college success story. What makes a student a success is simply setting the goal of graduating from college—and reaching that goal. It's time consuming to be an athlete. You have to travel and train, and also put the time in the classroom. If you leave Baylor with a degree, you've put the work in. There are no gimme degrees at Baylor.

I think any coach will tell you they have aspirations of national championships, which I was fortunate enough to win both as a player and as an assistant coach at Louisiana Tech. Nevertheless, you have to start as you do with a baby—crawl before you walk, set realistic goals. You think maybe down the road of winning the Big 12 title. You think about getting the school's first NCAA bid. You have to set realistic goals and go from there. Our immediate goal was to compete in the Big 12, compete with the top five or six teams in the conference, and get an NCAA bid. When Geno Auriemma took over at Connecticut I don't think he could have predicted that he was going to win a national championship after five or six years. I know I sure didn't.

That first year we made little things monumental. We played in a tournament in Boston at Boston University. Those were the first two games I ever coached for Baylor and we won them both, beating Miami of Ohio and Yale. While we were in Boston the Celtics' general manager at the time, Chris Wallace, gave us a tour of the FleetCenter (now the TD Banknorth Garden) and took us to see the team's locker room. I got the impression that a lot of the players had never been to such a venue or seen an NBA locker room. It was a genuine thrill for them to see Paul Pierce and Antoine Walker's jerseys hanging in their lockers.

I always try to mix some history or fun into a road trip. During the 2005–06 season, I scheduled a game against Army because I wanted our players to see West Point, and the truth be told, I wanted to see it as well. We spent three days in New York, seeing *The Lion King* on Broadway and winning the basketball game as well.

When we achieved our 15th win that first year we had a celebration because it meant that we would not have a losing season. When we beat our first ranked opponent we celebrated again. It was big. All along the way, we acknowledged all accomplishments. I was a realist. You have to have real expectations and I had them—we had them. Each year our expectations progressed and incredibly each year we met them.

"It was so much fun to come to practice every day that first year, knowing we were going to be playing at such a high level," Bruns said. "And we knew that she had played at a similar level and that she knew what she was talking about. Sometimes she would even join us in scrimmages and you could tell she could still play. She was tough. Really tough. You never knew what words were going to come out of her mouth. But she was a great person to be around. Everyone respected her. And she was always fair. We knew what she was coming in to do. We worked our rear ends off that first season. I would say she is the type of person you want to make proud of you."

One of my lasting memories of that first year was when all of the team and coaching staff gathered at the Student Life Center to watch the selection show for the NCAA Tournament on ESPN. We felt we had an excellent chance to be chosen in the field of 64. No Baylor women's team had ever played in the NCAA Tournament. Our record was 20–7, which we hoped was good enough for an at-large invitation given that we played in a tough conference and was ranked in the top 25 for most of the second half of the season. Everyone was wearing green and gold and there were so many fans there that people were leaning over the balcony on the second floor to get a better shot of the giant television.

Then came the moment: We were placed in the West Regional as the No. 8 seed and matched up against Arkansas in the first round. Arkansas was coached by Gary Blair, who I knew quite well because he was an assistant coach when I played at Louisiana Tech. As soon as the match-up was announced, all you could hear throughout the building were cries of "Sic 'em Bears." I remember getting patched into the ESPN feed and saying that we never anticipated going so far, so fast. All we wanted to do was lay a foundation that year. I also said it was a great day for Baylor women's basketball—and it was.

We lost our game to Arkansas. They were much more experienced and we were simply overmatched. We played as well as we could and as hard as we could, but it really didn't matter. They had better players and they had been to the Final Four three years earlier. This was all new to us—our first NCAA Tournament game.

Soon thereafter, Tom Stanton and I met for our annual evaluation session. "She said she didn't think we were going to be able to do it as fast as we did. But she also told me she thought there was still a long way to go," Stanton says.

When Stanton signed me he told me that he would be happy to renegotiate the deal once he was convinced the program was turned around and heading in the right direction. One season convinced him. He believed in acting preemptively and ripped up my contract, re-signing me to a new seven-year deal. He wanted to ensure that my coach's salary was commensurate with the salaries of the other top coaches in women's college basketball and he also wanted to drive home his point that he wanted the good coaches at Baylor to stick around.

8

Recruiting and Rules

Recruiting is the lifeblood of all programs. There are coaches who are better at recruiting than coaching on the floor and there are coaches who are better on the floor than at recruiting. You have to find the perfect balance and mix and you have to have assistant coaches that make you look good. I don't think any coach can say that he or she enjoys rejection, so I find it amusing when coaches say they enjoy recruiting. It's tough work.

Recruiting these days is absolutely mind-boggling, which combined with the standard game schedule makes college coaching a 12-month-a-year job. I have to make myself take a vacation each summer in August. In April and May, immediately after the season is over, we are still permitted to sign players or bring them to campus for a visit. In June, we conduct our basketball camps. We usually have three camps at Baylor: a two-day camp for elite players, a four-day overnight camp for individuals, and a half-day camp for younger players that lasts four days.

As coaches we make money from our camps, but it is not a primary source of income for any of us. And I'm going to do whatever I can to make sure it doesn't come to that. All colleges have camps and they are a source of income for the coaches. At some schools its all the coaches do in the summer. We did a lot of camps at Louisiana Tech, but I thought we conducted too many. I do not want my coaches to be burned out. They need to be rested for the month of July, which is our recruiting evaluation period. It is a very important month for making recruiting decisions.

A typical recruiting season starts when we attend tournaments and events that feature some of the best players in the country. The NCAA must sanction these events or we are not allowed to attend them. During the tournaments, coaches evaluate players. The rules are very clear: You are not permitted to speak to or have any contact with the players; you are only allowed to watch them play. We typically observe players from as young as 10 years old to players as old as 17. Coaches buy packets that consist of game schedules, rosters, players' home mailing addresses, and coaches' contact information. The average cost of a packet is $150, but they can run as high as $600.

Every college is usually represented at these tournaments or events. The players are of all ages and talents and we rotate from gym to gym watching them and their respective teams play. Of course, you notice the talented players who stand out. What you can't see at an early age are the girls who are going to develop and surpass the other girls because of their drive and their love of the game.

We don't sit down at our staff meetings and make sure someone covers the sixth and seventh graders. We focus on the high school kids. If along the way there's something sanctioned for junior high kids, and we don't have anything else scheduled, we may watch it. We all remember Damon Bailey, the kid from Indiana who committed to Bob Knight when he was in junior high school. There is always the chance that there might be another Damon Bailey out there.

We make sure we have files on each player in whom we have developed an interest. We send them questionnaires that mainly request biographical information. This is the only permissible way for us to initiate communication with recruits until their junior year of high school. We are allowed to watch recruits play five times during the scholastic calendar year. On September 1 of a student-athlete's junior year in high school, colleges are permitted to start sending them unlimited written correspondence. In August 2007, the NCAA outlawed text and instant messaging contact because it was taking up too much of their time. Student-athletes can come on unofficial visits to the university anytime, but those trips must be paid for by the student-athlete.

When a student is a senior she can make as many as five official visits to five campuses. The university pays for official visits. Additionally, colleges are permitted to call a student once a week and can arrange to visit her home and school during the designated contact period.

There are parts of recruiting that are enjoyable, such as getting to meet players and their families. However, when a 17- or 18-year-old has the power to dictate your livelihood, it's not fun. I don't chitchat on the phone for hours with a recruit. That's not me. I know I wouldn't want a coach imposing on my daughter's time. If a recruit needs 15 minutes of my time, I will give her that time. I will talk to her as long as I need to in order to get her to come to Baylor. But to keep a young lady on the phone for hours is selfish.

Most seniors choose to sign their scholarships with a college during the early signing period in November. Others wait until after their season is over and sign in April or May. When I was in high school I waited until the end of basketball season to sign with Louisiana Tech although I knew all along which college I was going to attend.

The recruiting calendar and coaching schedule are a balancing act during certain times of the year. At Baylor, our players work with our strength and conditioning coach when school starts in August. In September, NCAA rules allow us to do individual skill instruction with no more than four players at a time. Before our official practices start in mid-October, we can work with them up to two hours a week. This helps teaching the drills and the pace we will need in practice. Sometimes I have the players work out at 6:00 AM in order to instill discipline.

September is also the time of the year when we are permitted to make home visits to seniors in high school, so I have to sometimes work those visits around workouts at Baylor.

Academically, Baylor sells itself. From a basketball standpoint I tell recruits, "Look what we've done since we've been here. We started from scratch and we've worked our way up to respectability. If you walk across our campus and visit our facilities, you will quickly see that they are second to none. We don't take a back seat to anyone. The dorms are new. Many of the athletic facilities are new. Everything a student needs to be successful is right here and available to you."

From a coaching standpoint, I hope that a recruit knows my coaching style before I walk into her home. I am intense and I am going to challenge her. We have a job to do on that floor and we need to be prepared. I'm competitive and demand the same from my players. I will always defend, stand up for, and fight for my players and the program. I don't tolerate criticism of a player by fans or alumni. I'm the only one who can "get on them."

I'm happy to sit down and answer any questions the recruit and her family may have about Baylor, myself, and the team. I will discuss concerns regarding their daughter's potential basketball career. However, I am very clear that once I have signed a player, I will not deal with parents regarding basketball-related issues. I will never talk to them about their daughter's playing time. At this level you know that parents are not going to be happy all the time. I tell them, "I will talk to you about your daughter's health. I will talk to you about your daughter's education. I will talk to you if you need my help with something that happens at home, a death in the family, or anything else of that nature. But we will never sit down and have a conversation about playing time." I don't even have conversations with the players about playing time. When I talk to them it's about the areas they need to improve and how they can accomplish those goals.

I know some parents occasionally leave a game mad because their daughter hasn't played enough or was pulled out of a game. I understand their frustration, but I cannot allow myself to be approached about it. I wish after games I could hug more parents and have conversations with them, but I can't be put in that position. The greatest example a coach can be to a young person is to let them observe you coach and be resolute in your decisions.

When I am in a young lady's living room on a recruiting visit I tell her up front that scholarships are for one year and are renewable. The NCAA requires all coaches to explain this to a recruit. Schools usually renew each year, but a coach has the freedom not to renew. If a scholarship is not renewed, the player has the right to appeal to a committee that is comprised of faculty, not athletic personnel. Transferring happens often in collegiate athletics. I have had players transfer to other schools; I have even encouraged players to transfer. It is not a fun part of my job, but I believe in being honest with an athlete about her role and her future in the program.

(*left*) A sign of things to come? Always thinking pass-first even in a highchair.

(*right*) A sit-down family photo when I was four years old. My younger sister, Tammy, is on the left.

(*left*) Working on my ballhandling skills on the court in our backyard. I would play alone for hours on end.

(*left*) I started for much of my career at Louisiana Tech, but I was always into the game—whether I was on the floor or cheering from the bench. And only losing six times in four years, we usually had plenty to cheer about!

(*below*) Getting the lowdown from Coach Barmore with Pam Gant listening in. Notice the pigtails and the uniforms—short sleeves and collars for the Lady Techsters.

(*left*) I'm driving by seven-foot two-inch Hall of Famer Uljana Semjonova during a game in Russia. (Don't look at my right foot!)

(*below*) The 1984 Olympic Gold Medal Team. It was disappointing not to have played the Russians who boycotted, but I felt we were so good we would have beaten them anyway.

In 15 years as an assistant coach under Leon Barmore at Louisiana Tech, we won more than 400 games, including a national championship. There were plenty of opportunities to cheer, including this one.

Even before Makenzie was born, we hired Annie Talbert to help us with childcare. She remains close to me and the kids to this day.

Hey ref, how could you have missed that?
Some people say I tend to be a bit animated on the sidelines.

Hand signals are necessary to get play information to the players. We have many games where the fans are so vocal that it would be impossible to call plays audibly.

The players with the NCAA trophy flanked by the two Big 12 Conference trophies (regular season and tournament championship) that we won in 2005.

In New York City to receive the prestigious Winged Foot Award after winning the 2005 National Championship. Roy Williams of North Carolina joins me.

(*left*) It seemed like the whole city of Waco came out to celebrate our 2005 National Championship. Each player had a Corvette to ride in! It was wonderful to be able to share the championship with so many people.

A mother-daughter moment with Makenzie early on in my time at Baylor. Kramer sits behind his sister.

Makenzie, me, and Kramer on the Baylor campus with our chocolate lab, CoCo.

Will the success we've had make Baylor a more appealing place? It will open some doors, but I don't think a young lady is going to magically wake up one day and say, "Oh, I want to go to Baylor." There simply are too many great programs.

However, we have been able to get into homes that we couldn't get into when we first got to Baylor. We still have to continue to be selective and we have to make sure we don't waste our time in recruiting. I don't like coming in second and third. Some coaches get a kick out of being in somebody's top five. That doesn't do much for me. I want to get into the mix and get the players that can come and help us compete and win.

Some of a coach's greatest joys and biggest disappointments come from recruiting. We are now able to recruit on the national level instead of just regionally or locally and that shows how far our program has come.

I always say that you don't coach speed and quickness—you recruit it. I'd like to say that we heavily recruited Sophia Young, who was fast and quick and became an All-American at Baylor, but we didn't. Her story is not the norm; it is a recruiting fairytale. You can coach a lifetime and never win a national title. You can recruit a lifetime and never have something like her story happen. Nevertheless, it did happen, and boy, am I glad it did.

Sophia was a foreign exchange student at Evangel Christian School in Shreveport, Louisiana. Jennifer Roberts, one of my assistants, is from Shreveport and also attended Evangel Christian. Jennifer's brother was in school with Sophia and her father, Bo, started an AAU women's basketball program in Shreveport.

Sophia played for Evangel Christian her sophomore year but was required to sit out a year because of Louisiana state high school regulations. She didn't play her junior year, but she did attend a summer basketball camp at Louisiana Tech. She was looking to improve her game and ended up contacting Jennifer's father for help. At first he turned her down because he wasn't coaching anymore. But after her fourth phone call, his heart told him that he needed to meet this young lady. He watched her play and casually mentioned to his daughter that there might be a diamond in the rough right in her own backyard.

Jennifer passed the information along to me. I said, "Jennifer, if she was any good and she was at Louisiana Tech's camp, don't you think they'd be all over her?" She said, "Yeah, you're right." We dismissed it. Later, Jennifer mentioned Sophia again and we decided to drive to Shreveport and watch her work out. I walked into the gym and within five minutes of watching her play, I said, "Oh my goodness." I said to Jennifer, "We've got to keep this hush-hush until we can sign her." We could see that she didn't know the game very well and that she didn't possess a single post move. Nevertheless, we could also see her quickness, her leaping ability, and above all, her potential.

I couldn't help but wonder why Louisiana Tech hadn't tried to sign her. I found out after the fact that some people at Louisiana Tech had the same reaction. When I was at Tech we always tried to make sure that we recruited the best players in the state. I called some coaches who worked their camp and asked them what they thought of Sophia. One coach told me she was very good and was surprised that Louisiana Tech had not recruited her. Another coach wasn't as sure about her or her potential. I was trying to get a feel for her, but I never could. I guess she was overlooked at camp because no other major university ever seriously tried to recruit her. I sure thought this kid was for real, so we signed her as quickly as we could, in November of her senior year.

With Sophia one thing helped enormously: She had not had a lot of coaching before she came to Baylor. When something is new, you absorb it. She came to us and we basically taught her all she ever learned. I didn't have to push Sophia. The thing we had to do was get her to save what we like to call "wasted energy." In other words, in practice she would do things she didn't need to do, like fronting a post player five feet from the basket. She had so much energy that we had to rein it in. We also had to teach her post moves. She had a tremendous work ethic, an ability to concentrate for a long period of time, incredible stamina, and she could play tired.

The Young signing proved to be a fortunate one in terms of timing because she emerged as one of the state's best prep players as a senior at Evangel Christian. Before that season Baylor was the only major college program to recruit Young. Her other pursuers were

Nicholls State in Thibodeaux, Louisiana, a member of the Southland Conference; Centenary College in Shreveport, Louisiana, a member of the Mid-Continent Conference; Arkansas-Little Rock, a member of the Sun Belt Conference; and Arkansas-Monticello of the Gulf South Conference. None of those women's programs had ever participated in an NCAA game. Fortunately, Young chose Baylor. She said she saw a basketball program on the upswing.

In her final season at Evangel Christian, Young averaged 26 points and 13.3 rebounds a game and set a school record by scoring 48 points against Ruston High School. She was named All-State and All-District and was selected to play in the Louisiana All-Star Game.

You can recruit for years and never have a story like Abiola Wabara. Her aunt, Phoebe Wabara, was attending the Truett Seminary at Baylor. Phoebe kept emailing Johnny Derrick, one of my assistant coaches, about a niece living in Parma, Italy who was a very good basketball player. Well, as you can imagine, we get these kinds of emails all the time from parents and grandparents who think their children and grandchildren are the greatest things since sliced bread. However, something about this email stood out to Johnny and he arranged for Abi to stop by for a visit when she came to the United States to see her aunt.

When I shook her hand I said to myself, "Wow, big hands. That's good." She had a very strong, muscular body. That was good, too. But we couldn't work her out because it was against NCAA rules. I asked her about her playing in Italy and if she knew a professional player named Janice Lawrence. I told her that I had played with Janice at Louisiana Tech for four years.

After Abi and her aunt left, I picked up the phone and called Janice. We hadn't been in contact for awhile, but she was a friend and an ex-teammate and I knew she'd be straight with me. Janice had seen Abi play. They even knew each other. I asked Janice to describe Abi's style of play. Then I said, "Janice, I'm trying to build a program at Baylor. Can she help me?" Janice said she could.

Without ever seeing her play, work out, or practice I signed her. Abi had to be cleared by the NCAA and she was red-shirted as a freshman. As part of the NCAA ruling she also had to miss the first seven games of the next season because she played club ball in Italy. The paperwork was rather involved to get her on the court, but it all ended up working out.

That's the side of recruiting that rarely happens. These two young ladies literally fell into our laps. They were so many miles away from home. Sophia's mother, who lived in St. Vincent in the Grenadines, finally got to see her daughter play during the 2005 Final Four. It was a very emotional moment for both of them. I can still remember Sophia running into the stands to give her mother a big hug after we beat Michigan State. Sophia and Abi played important roles on our team and had great years together at Baylor.

✦

To say that Young and Wabara played important roles in leading Baylor to the national championship would be a dramatic understatement. Young had the best freshman season ever for a Baylor woman and became the first freshman in Big-12 Conference history to lead the league in rebounding. In the last game of her freshman season, the WNIT Final against Auburn, she hauled in 25 rebounds, a school and conference record.

Young became the first two-time Kodak All-American at Baylor; the Big 12 Conference's all-time leading scorer and rebounder; and only the second woman at Baylor since the NCAA took over sponsorship of woman's basketball in 1982 to finish her career with more than 2,000 points and 1,000 rebounds.

✦

I always tell recruits what I consider to be my rules for behavior at Baylor. I only have a few rules concerning a players' appearance. When we travel on the road I want them to dress in what I call "casual nice." This means a nice pair of blue jeans that have been ironed and a good, tucked-in shirt. I haven't had a problem with the dress code; the assistant coaches let the players know what is appropriate and what is not. Sometimes we permit the players to wear warm-ups on trips depending on how tired we are or where we are going. The main thing is that

I want them to represent Baylor in a positive light. I don't want people to see our team and say, "They look like a bunch of thugs." I don't allow do-rags or wrap-around-your-head stuff. I tell them, "You can sleep in it, but I don't want to see it."

In this regard, I can't control tattoos either. Kids usually have them before they come to Baylor. I give them my lecture: Do you realize that its permanent? Do you realize when you're 80 years old and rocking your grandbaby what it's going to look like? You are going to have saggy skin and it is definitely not going to look like it does today.

Another thing I can't control off the court is piercings. On the court, they aren't allowed to wear any jewelry. I tell them I don't think that nose rings or pierced eyebrows look good but that's just the old coach talking. They let me tease them but ultimately I have no control over them—and I would never try.

Occasionally I set a curfew. I'm lenient when school starts, but when the season begins, they will have a curfew if I think it is necessary. It may be midnight during the week and 1:00 AM. on the weekends. It depends on how they're doing on the floor. I have the seniors, captains, and coaches call and check on them. And I always tell them, "Just when you least expect it, there will be a knock on your door." Sometimes curfews mean all they have to do is be in their dorm room or apartment by the designated time. Really, when you think about it, why would you want to be out on the street after midnight anyway? You aren't going to be up to anything good on the streets of Waco, Texas after midnight.

In my fourth year at Baylor, I dismissed my starting point guard, Ebony Jackson, because she continued to break team rules. Her dismissal came at the worst possible time—right in the middle of conference play. She had numerous chances to correct the situation, but it never got better. The punishments never seemed to change anything. I am a stickler for rules and discipline. You had better be on time. You had better represent Baylor in a professional manner. You had better attend classes because, after all, you are there to get an education and a degree. I know there are a lot of coaches and programs where they actually assign one of the assistants or someone else in the program to make sure a player gets to class. If I ever have to do that, I will get out of the business. I won't have an assistant coach waking up a player and walking her to class. What lesson are we teaching when we do that for a player?

I understand that people might think I threw Ebony out on the street, but I tried to encourage her to transfer to a junior college or a community college and finish up at another four-year school. But she didn't and I never heard from her again.

I also dismissed Monique Jones from the team just before the start of the 2005–06 season, also for violating a team rule. She was arrested by the local police and I will never forget seeing her on television in an orange jump suit. It broke my heart. When I spoke with Monique she was remorseful and contrite and knew she had embarrassed herself and the team.

But I dismissed her immediately because I felt she had compromised the integrity of the program and the university. It was very hard for me because Monique was one of my all-time favorite players. She was a team player. She always encouraged others, yet she also wanted to play herself. Dismissing her was so difficult because I knew in my heart that she was a good person and a good student.

I always stress to the team, "Don't ever embarrass yourself, your university, your coaches, or your team. And after weighing all the facts, I felt I had to dismiss her. However, I believed in her so much that I spent four hours the next day calling coaches trying to find her another school. Finally, Coach Rick Pietri at the University of South Alabama agreed to take her. Monique sat out the 2005–06 season because of NCAA rules regarding transferring, but she had two years of eligibility remaining at the start of the 2006–07 season.

Everyone's rules are not the same as mine and I think that's why the University of South Alabama was willing to take Monique. It was the timing of her arrest as much as anything else. We just had our first team meeting of the season and reviewed all of the team rules. I told every coach that I called that I would not be bothering him or her if I didn't think this young lady deserved a second chance. With you, she will be starting new. With me, she won't. I had to look at the players on my team and let

137

them know that I didn't tolerate infractions. If I did the issue would not go away and I might have to deal with it again. You don't want to look at your players knowing that they're thinking: She screwed up, she broke a team rule, and yet Coach Mulkey is letting her back on the team.

After she got to South Alabama, I periodically called to check up on Monique because she is special to me. She is a good person who made a bad decision. She would have played a very big part in our program. Many coaches have asked me if I would have dismissed her if she was a starter. I respond, if you're asking me that, you don't know me very well. Monique was going to play significant minutes for us and could have become a starter. (She did actually end up being a starter in her first year of eligibility at South Alabama.) That wouldn't have changed my mind. Her dismissal was based solely on the facts, the seriousness of the crimes, and the arrest. I am not saying I will dismiss every player that gets arrested. The seriousness of the arrest and the facts of the case are what will determine my decision. That's what I did with Monique. I put my reputation on the line for her and I would not have done it if she wasn't a good person. She made a mistake—and we all make mistakes.

9

Coaching Philosophy

Coaching is a wonderful profession. It's a profession that has the highest of highs and lowest of lows. It's also a profession that everybody can scrutinize. I always say that coaching is like teaching but with one significant difference: Coaches are on a bigger stage. If a teacher has a bad teaching day, the only people who know about it are the students in the class. If a coach has a bad day; makes the wrong call or substitution; or doesn't use a timeout, it has more impact because thousands of people are watching. The visibility that comes with coaching can be both good and bad.

Ultimately, all of the decisions fall on you when you are a head coach. That's the biggest difference between being an assistant coach and a head coach. That and the fact that you sleep better as an assistant. However, I'm big on one thing—my assistants have input in my decisions. Sometimes they like to tease me by saying it doesn't matter what suggestions they make because I'm still going to do what I want to do anyway. I remember making those same statements to Coach Barmore when I was an assistant at Louisiana Tech. Nevertheless, I think they realize how much I value their input. After all, I walked in an assistant's shoes for 15 years.

When we're at practice I only want the assistant coaches to talk when they're absolutely certain that the way they are teaching is the same way I would teach. I have no problem with them interjecting, hollering, or saying something to a player. I support my coaches. If they say something wrong or make a mistake I will not embarrass them. I'll jump in and say, "What Coach means is" and cover for him or her. I want the coaches' opinions. I want them to feel free to tell me what they think. It takes working together for some time to be able to read each other and not get your feelings hurt. We can have knockdown drag out arguments in staff meetings or agree to disagree on something like recruiting but that's where it should stay—behind closed doors. A sense of loyalty has to come into play and everyone must realize that we're all fighting for the same goals. I'm sure my assistant coaches have had moments when they've been fed up with what I am saying, but they also know it's just me being Kim and they shouldn't take it personally. I'm intense. I coach in the moment. I stand by my hiring decisions and I am proud of all my assistant coaches.

The majority of what I do as a coach is what I learned from Leon Barmore at Louisiana Tech and Pat Summitt in the Olympics. They're hard-nosed, aggressive, get in your face type coaches carved from the same mold. My style of coaching comes from having played for them. I have a natural toughness about me that I was born with but also developed further when I played for Coach Summitt and Coach Barmore. They make you tough.

Coach Summitt and Coach Barmore are both unbelievable leaders. They demand the utmost. I didn't find it difficult playing for either Coach Barmore or Coach Summitt. Both are very vocal. Both make you exert yourself beyond what you think you are capable of giving. Both demand your respect. I never called any of my coaches by their first name. Pat wanted us to call her Pat, but I never did. It was always Coach Summitt.

Coach Summitt emphasized playing weights and made me lose about 10 pounds after she selected me to play on the Olympic team. I wasn't the only one who had to do it, most of the team did. She wanted her players to be a certain weight and you had better be at that weight. The truth is, I played about 10 pounds over my "ideal" weight while I was at Louisiana Tech. Coach Barmore never thought it affected my play, so he wasn't overly bothered by it.

When you are around strong personalities like theirs for as long as I was, it rubs off on you. But you can't change your own personality. You are who you are. If you can incorporate a coaching style with your own personality, then you are going to be successful. Demanding each players' best is what all coaches should do. I have never wanted to be around mediocrity.

Sure, you can do a drill at half-speed and look good, but if you don't stay on them when they're freshman, they will still be at that same pace when they're sophomores. You try to teach them to find something inside themselves that they didn't think or know they had.

I'll be the first one to admit that I've made numerous mistakes at Baylor. There are things I wish I could undo. Nevertheless, I live and learn. I might handle a situation that happened my first year at Baylor a little differently because I have more experience now. Looking back, I can second-guess some of my reactions and decisions. Could I have been a little bit gentler? Should I have been a little more demanding? All I hope is that the players I coach know when they leave Baylor they've been challenged to reach a level they never thought they could reach. If they know that, then I've done my job as their coach.

I freely admit that my personality is not for everyone. I may be too tough for some players. As I said before, I played with emotion; I coach with emotion. I am brutally honest with the players and tell them they cannot take the things I say personally. They know that I'm trying to make them better players and teach them how to play hard. That's what it's all about—playing hard. I am motivated by challenge and an "I'll-show-you" mentality. My hope is that this will motivate them as well—the challenge to be the best they can be.

There were things I went through as a player years ago, particularly from a conditioning standpoint, that players today could not endure. We ran a ton of suicides, which are drills where you start at the baseline and run to the foul line and back, then to halfcourt and back, then to the other foul line and back, and then to the other baseline and back. Coach Barmore used to make us run these for long periods of time, sometimes even after we won! I remember one instance involving Pam Kelly, a three-time All-American who was one of Coach Barmore's favorites. He never wanted to upset Pam too much and we always teased her about it. But during one practice, we were told to start running suicides. Back then you didn't complain. You couldn't complain. But I was exhausted. I don't ever remember being that tired in my life and Coach Barmore was all over us. This was his first college job and he was young and intense. We were running for what seemed like an eternity when we pleaded with Pam to start pretending like she was hyperventilating. We figured that because Coach Barmore liked Pam so much, he would stop the suicides if he saw his favorite player hyperventilating. It worked. Coach Barmore knows the real story now and he got a kick out of it when I told him the truth. But he also told me he had a very good reason for liking Pam Kelly: She was good for almost 20 points and 10 rebounds every game.

Coaches don't have to do as much conditioning on the floor these days. Players usually report to practice pretty well conditioned after having worked with strength and conditioning coaches during the summer. The modern-day athlete has probably never had to endure a practice after a game, let alone run suicides after a game. Of course, NCAA rules don't allow it, but it would be interesting to see the look on all their faces if I told them we were going to practice after a game.

I'm still as hard-nosed and disciplined as ever; that is never going to change. I think I'm pretty consistent with who I am, but through experience, I think how I react to the players has changed. They don't know about my era and I don't want to bore them with stories about the "old days." However, I do want them to know the history of our game. I share stories and read articles to them. I've always been motivated by intense coaches and I will always believe that one's chief want and desire in life is to find that someone who can make you do what you're capable of doing—and then some. Coach Barmore and Coach Summitt did that for me. I try to do the same thing for my players.

I have been asked if with my personality I could play for any coach. I played for Leon Barmore. He was tough. I played for Pat Summitt. She was no different than Coach Barmore. I could have even played for Bob Knight. I have that toughness and grit about me. As a player, I may not like or agree with what a coach is saying, but I always did what was asked of me. I would never open my mouth as a player, because that would not be showing the proper respect for the coach. In my day, if a coach told you to jump you would ask "How high?" I will admit that maybe under your breath you might say some ugly things, but you would never say anything directly to the coach.

Every player likes a pat on the back. When I played, one pat on the back lasted me about six months and meant something. Nowadays, players want pats on the back every day. That's a big change for me. Today, young people's needs are different. They need constant reassurance. I work really hard to do more of that for them. I think the kids require more pats on the back now because our society is so much more of a what-have-you-done-for-me-lately society. We provide more to our young people than was ever provided to us. It's easy to buy a computer today. It's easier to buy a car today. Everything is easier today. I don't know why. I just think there are no consequences for actions anymore. We don't hold kids accountable for little things anymore. If you missed curfew back when I played, it was horrible. Today they laugh at you—you're going to suspend me because I missed curfew? There are fewer ground rules.

I guess it's the changing of the times. Now, it's easier for kids to play a computer game than to go outside, get sweaty, and shoot 100 free throws and jump shots. Kids think, "I'll do that at practice for two hours in an air-conditioned gym and that will be fine." We didn't have computers as kids. We didn't have Play Station, X-Box, and all these hand-held gadgets. You went outside and played. You shot a ball. You rode a bike. Kids just don't do that anymore. Nowadays, they put their feet up, eat a bag of Cheetos, and play on the computer. When they get bored they turn on the Play Station. Then they send a few text messages on their cell phones. There are just too many things for them to do. Kids today are over-stimulated and under-challenged.

Players all think they're pretty good and that's all right. I don't want them to think they're not. My job when they come to Baylor is to break them down and build them back up. You have to clear their minds of whatever system they were playing in high school and put them into your system. In high school if a kid had a bad day she probably was still the best player on her team and could coast through. You can't do that at this level.

I have been lucky at Baylor to have had players who bought into what we are doing as an organization. In all my years at the university, there was only one time when I kicked a player out of practice. The player was Stasha Richards, who played three years for me. It was my first year and I was trying to send a message to the entire team. I wanted Stasha to raise her game. I thought there was another gear she had that she just wasn't using—and she could shift into if she set her mind to it. I wasn't sure if she knew she had that extra gear. I told her, "I know you've got more. I know you can give more. So get out of here and come back when you are ready to give it to me." I was trying to set an example, set a tone. I thought I

146

could challenge her and that she could handle it. She came back the next day, which told me she could. Stasha is now in the coaching profession at the collegiate level. When we run into each other recruiting, we talk and laugh about me throwing her out of practice.

Each day before we take the floor for practice, I write a "Thought for the Day" on the board in the locker room. The thought can range from a motivational saying to something more intense that might relate to something the team did or how they played the previous practice or game. Most of these thoughts were acquired while I was at Louisiana Tech and are kept in a special notebook. One of my favorites is, "If What You Did Yesterday Still Looks Big to You Today, Then You Haven't Done Much Today." Some others are "The Real Test of a Player Comes when Things Don't Go to Suit Her" and "Today I Gave All I Had. What I've Kept, I've Lost Forever."

We start practice with the same routine, every time. We stretch, do lay-ups, and shoot short jump shots off the glass. The next 40 minutes are spent doing team drills. Then we normally split up by positions. The post players are working on one end of the floor while the guards are working on the other end of the floor. We try to spend 20 to 30 minutes on offense and another 20 to 30 minutes on defense. Practices generally last about two to two and a half hours. However, if I have a young team I may need to keep them a little longer. In January and February the practices are shortened. We keep a log of all the time we spend and we submit it to our compliance office. This is a requirement because the NCAA rules only allow a certain number of hours for practice each week.

We scrimmage a lot before the season starts, and when we scrimmage, I often have my players play against a group of male students. I like it. It gives me an opportunity to watch five players instead of 10. I can concentrate on just my players. If they are going against each other I must focus on both offense and defense and we're probably not going to get better at either one. We call these Baylor students our "Dream Team." We haven't gone down to the recreational center and said, "Hey, c'mon over." The men have to be cleared by the NCAA, just like a recruited athlete. They have to have the grades. This has become a hot issue with the NCAA even though most women's programs do it. In my opinion, I hope it's never stopped because it is a positive for my players and for the men, too.

My standard routine for coaching on home game days is to have our shoot-around for an hour from twelve o'clock to one o'clock or from one o'clock to two o'clock depending on schedules and classes. There is a required pre-game meal, catered at the gym. I don't eat with the players. The girls are then required to stay in their rooms for 90 minutes. They get taped and receive whatever medical treatment they need at least one hour before the game. I then require them to be on the floor one hour prior to game time and shoot on their own for 10 or 15 minutes but no more. They usually get to the Ferrell Center around 4:45 PM for a 7:00 PM game.

In the afternoon I get my hair done, which usually takes about 20 minutes. Then I go home and relax. I leave my house at 5:30 PM and drive to the Ferrell Center, which takes about 20 minutes. This schedule gets me there about an hour before the game. I go straight to my office and soon the Baylor radio announcer arrives for the pre-game interview. We go over details from the last game and look ahead to that night's opponent. After he leaves, I stay in my office and think over what we've worked on that week and what situations may arise during the game. For about 20 minutes I concentrate and focus on the impending game. Then I head to the locker room.

While the players are doing their pre-game warm-ups on the floor, I write on the locker room board reminding the team what we're going to do offensively and defensively. I may add a couple of motivational comments, such as the ones mentioned earlier. Then I leave and go down the hall to the training room. When the players return to the locker room, they read what is written on the board.

About seven or eight minutes before the players take the court, I return to the locker room and review with them what I have written. Then either one of the assistant coaches or I lead us in a prayer. We're a private school, so we're allowed to pray and I have never had a player object to it. Part of the reason could be because Baylor is a faith-based institution. You certainly don't have to be a Baptist to go there, anymore than you have to be a Methodist to go to SMU or a Catholic to go to Notre Dame. You don't even have to be a Christian to go to Baylor. Nevertheless, we say a prayer before taking the court; it's just something I feel comfortable with.

Finally, we recite our little chant: "All for One, One for All. Go Baylor. 1, 2, 3, We Believe!" Then the players run onto the floor to the cheering crowd. I stay in the locker room for another three or four minutes trying to time it so that I am on the court only two minutes before the start of the game. I learned this from Coach Barmore. I asked him why he came to the floor so late and he said that it allowed him to stay focused. I know it allows me to avoid speaking to people. I don't want to be rude, but at that point, I'm so focused. If I come out early, I'm going to look around, talk to people, acknowledge people, and maybe allow my mind to wander away from what I'm there to do.

I am usually not on the floor when the "National Anthem" is played. I am more patriotic than many people realize. I feel it's important that everyone stand at attention and put their hands over their hearts when the anthem is played.

At halftime the coaches meet in a room down the hall from the locker room and go over things. It can be intense or it can be laid back. It all depends on how the first half was played. After the coaches meet, I address the team in the locker room. Sometimes, I will address them in a "Come to Jesus" way, very short and to the point. Most of the time, I review things that we have to do better and I make any necessary changes. The changes could be defensively; they could be reviewing a few plays that we haven't run yet; or just telling them the areas requiring improvement, such as rebounding, turnovers, defense, and the like.

Sometimes, at the most intense moments, I may go in and write one word on the board and walk out. An example of what I might write is words like "Relax," "Defense," or "Will to Win." It's a feel you get. It's not a ritual. It's not the same every game. The pre-game is a ritual. The feel and flow of the game dictates what goes on during halftime.

After the game, I may not have a lot to say in the locker room. Again it's a feeling. But I always close with the Lord's Prayer. We hold hands in a circle and I sometimes ask a player to start the prayer. Then I go to the media room with two players. After I've addressed the media, I do the post-game radio show.

This is my routine and it has been the same for the last seven years.

10

One Long, Dark Summer

✺

In the late spring of 2003, Baylor's athletic director, Tom Stanton, was in his office at the university when he took a telephone call from the men's basketball coach, Dave Bliss. The next six words he heard—"We don't know where Patrick is"—changed his life and the lives of many in the Baylor community.

"Patrick" was Patrick Dennehy, a summer school student and basketball player who had transferred to Baylor after playing two seasons for the University of New Mexico. No one had seen or heard from him in days.

Soon thereafter, Stanton had what he later called "the most difficult phone conversation of my life" when he reached Dennehy's mother, Valorie Brabazon, and told her that her son was missing.

Dennehy was missing for more than a month before his body was discovered in a gravel pit. A six-foot ten-inch center who had dreams of playing in the NBA, Dennehy was shot twice in the head, once above the right ear and once in the neck area. A Baylor teammate and recent roommate of Dennehy's, Carlton Dotson, was arrested and charged with the killing. More than a year later, Dotson pleaded guilty and was sentenced to 35 years in prison even though his attorney thought his client was mentally ill. "It was an unbelievably tragic set of circumstances that you could not in your wildest dreams ever imagine," Stanton said. "It was something that turned everyone's life upside down and put everything in turmoil at the university."

As unimaginably horrific as the murder was, it was not a stand-alone incident in the men's basketball program. These kinds of monumental tragedies rarely are. Bliss, despite having just signed a six-year contract, was forced to resign the day after Dennehy's funeral. Information surfaced that he violated NCAA regulations by channeling money to Dennehy and another player for their tuitions because there were no scholarships available. He also told one of his assistants and some of the players to lie to investigators and say that Dennehy was a drug dealer. This was discovered only because one of Bliss' assistants secretly tape-recorded some of the conversations. University President Robert B. Sloan, Jr. said of Bliss, "I am outraged not only by his own deception but his efforts to enlist players and assistant coaches in this scheme." Additionally, it was learned that failed drug tests by other players had gone unreported.

On August 8, Sloan announced the resignation of both Bliss and Tom Stanton. The athletic director was forced to resign the same day as the disgraced Bliss, even though the school and its investigators went out of their way to note that Stanton had no knowledge of Bliss' activities. Stanton was the sacrificial lamb. He still lives in Waco

The scandal and the national media attention it received had a tremendous impact on the Baylor community. The story, as it unfolded over a period of months, garnered prominent headlines. Hard as that was, it was left to the other athletic programs at the institution to pick up the pieces and try to return to life as normal.

In the fall of 2003, I challenged my players during our first team meeting to be the shining light for the athletic department. I think we accomplished that. Baylor had never reached the Sweet 16 of the NCAA Tournament, but we did that year. For us, it was exciting. For the school, it was exciting. It was just one more step that we needed to take as a program.

What I'll never understand is how my office door was 10 feet away from one of the worst tragedies that ever happened in the history of college athletics and I knew nothing about it. It hurt a lot of people. Lives were changed and the repercussions rippled throughout the university.

My feeling was that it could have happened at any college, anywhere. I was just so sorry that it happened at all. It was so very sad for the families involved and all the people that were hurt. I saw the resignation of a very good man in Tom Stanton, the athletic director who hired me. I knew it hurt him to resign because he loved his job and he loved Baylor University. The incident affected innocent people who ultimately lost their jobs. Even President Sloan was targeted.

There were so many negatives, and for a while, it was difficult to get around them. Every day the parking lots were full of news crews from all over the country. There was always some new development or twist in the story. It just seemed to go on and on and on.

We discussed it as a coaching staff, but for the two to three hours we were on the floor at practice, we never talked about it. I mentioned it to the players only once, shortly after the incident happened. I asked them if they were all right and if I needed to call any of their parents. The paths of the two programs crossed because they were athletes playing the same sport, but I only had one player on my team that really knew Patrick Dennehy well enough to spend time with him.

We had a job to do as coaches. Every coach at Baylor University had to do his or her job and do it well. None of us had anything to do with what happened, yet we were the ones left to defend the university and our own programs. We had to roll up our sleeves and get back to work.

It was as if we made a conscious effort to say, "Look, there are a lot of good things happening at Baylor and there are many more to come." We won the NCAA championship in men's tennis. The women's basketball team was making significant strides. We had a terrific softball team. Both the baseball and track teams were continuing their winning traditions. That's what I tried to convey, although I'm not sure it ever stopped being an issue until after we won the NCAA championship.

Did it affect us? Of course it did. It affected everybody. It affected our recruiting. It affected donations to the university. It affected our alumni. How could it not? Nevertheless, we had to keep on working and hope that time would help all of us.

What helped our program was getting to the Sweet 16 for the first time since the university joined the NCAA. Winning helped cure a lot of negatives, or it at least diverted attention to something more positive.

The one area where it really affected us was recruiting. I felt it in every home I visited during the recruiting period. There were some recruits that we should have had a chance to bring to Baylor and it just didn't happen. In my mind, there was some reason why and that must have been it. It just wasn't hip or cool to consider Baylor at that particular point in time. I don't think it was personal. Recruits didn't associate me or my coaches with what happened, but Baylor wasn't generating a positive vibration and I could feel it.

I don't recall ever being personally told what to say about it—whether to bring it up or avoid it altogether. It was always there, however. No one ever hung up the phone on me just because I was calling from Baylor, but I was often asked to explain what happened. Parents wanted to know how closely the women's program interacted with the men's program. A lot of people didn't realize that the men's and women's programs, while physically separated by just a hallway, were actually very independent from each other.

I appreciated the questions and answered every one. If Baylor was recruiting my daughter, I would have asked those same questions. I felt a part of the healing process was making people understand that this wasn't a true picture of the university. The incident was terrible, but it could have happened at any university in the country.

Rarely does anyone around the university talk about the tragedy anymore unless, of course, the media asks questions. It's not going to define Baylor University. We are the oldest institution of higher learning in the State of Texas and we are not going to allow one tragedy to taint our university forever. That's the approach I took and that's the approach our players took.

One thing you learn in coaching, whether its from being rejected by a recruit or losing a tough game, is that you have to move on. You remember what happened and why it happened, but you move on. The one time it's hard to move on is when the loss is tough and it comes in a final game.

One such loss for me was during the 2002 NCAA Tournament. We had beaten Bucknell in the first round game and were playing Drake at home in the second round game. It was an overflow crowd of 10,074, at the time a record for a women's game at the Ferrell Center. We lost the game, 76–72.

There were many games at Baylor that we won but probably shouldn't have. We have had so many moments of excitement and excellence. The Drake loss was a tough one for me. In my opinion, we had more talent and we were supposed to win. We were the higher seeded team. We were playing on our home court. Sheila Lambert and Danielle Crockrom were seniors. It was the perfect setting for a home-court advantage and we didn't get it done. It was such a helpless feeling. Drake had an answer for everything we did. I felt personally responsible, because as the head coach, I couldn't get us over the hump. Most coaches take losses hard. It's harder to get over a tough loss than it is to exult after a big win, but each year I get better at not dwelling on the losses for too long. You have to move on to the next game.

We finished 24–8 in the season following the Patrick Dennehy tragedy. We were the No. 4 seed in the Midwest region and traveled to Albuquerque, New Mexico for our first two games of the tournament. We won the first game over Loyola Marymount and went on to beat Florida in the second game.

From there we advanced to the Sweet 16 for the first time in the history of the women's program. The site was

Norman, Oklahoma and the opponent was Tennessee, the top seed in the region. It was the first time in the school's history that Baylor played Tennessee and it was the first time that I coached against Pat Summitt. I thought that the last-second loss to North Carolina in the 1994 NCAA championship game was as low as I would ever feel as a coach. Well, that was nothing compared to how I felt after the Tennessee game.

We played well and had a double-digit lead in the second half before Tennessee came back and tied the score. With about 10 seconds left in the game, we had possession of the ball and I called a timeout, hoping that we would get the last shot. That way we would either win the game or go into overtime. I told our players that if we got into trouble they should call a timeout because we still had one left. None of that happened. We didn't get off the last shot. We didn't call a timeout. We turned the ball over.

Our point guard, Jessika Stratton, who was playing in what turned out to be her last game for Baylor, lost the ball. Then Shyra Ely, a player for Tennessee, missed a lay-up. The ball bounced off the rim and there was a scramble for a long rebound between Jessika and Tasha Butts from Tennessee. Then the horn sounded. I felt as if we'd dodged a big bullet. I thought the game was going into overtime.

To our amazement the referee called a foul on our player instead, putting two-tenths of a second back on the clock. It was a terrible call. People were screaming. Tasha Butts had a one-and-one. As she was shooting her free throws, I knew that with two-tenths of a second left in the game and the fact that we needed to go the full length of the court, we had absolutely no chance of getting off a decent shot or winning the game. We didn't. Tasha made both shots and we lost the game, 71–69.

As I shook hands with Pat Summitt after the game I said, "Congratulations Coach. But there's no way a game should end like that. That was a horrible call." Pat didn't respond nor did I expect her to. After all, what was she supposed to say? It wasn't her fault.

It is my understanding that the game's officiating crew was not allowed to advance or call any more games in the NCAA Tournament that year. I've also learned that at officiating clinics the ending of the Baylor-Tennessee game is often used to teach officials. I hope the lesson is called "How NOT to End a Game."

In the locker room after the game I was horrible. I didn't have the words to comfort Jessika Stratton. Nothing prepares you for a situation like that. I wish I could take back the way I acted and responded, but I can't. I like to think I am in control but this time I just wasn't. I was crying. I was throwing water bottles. I was so hurt and angry. I should have been comforting Jessika, but I couldn't even comfort myself. I really felt for the players, who were all crying. All I could think of doing was gathering everyone around, saying The Lord's Prayer, and getting out of Dodge.

If I'm ever in that situation again, and I hope I'm not, I like to think that I will act differently. I was not in control and I later apologized to the team. I also had a private meeting with Jessika and apologized to her. Many times I have publicly acknowledged that I was not a very good leader in the locker room after that game.

The season did two things. It gave us the mental strength to forge ahead to the next year and it shone a positive light on Baylor University after all the tragedy and trauma we went through the year before.

"I love Baylor University. People say you go to college for four years but, for me, Baylor is a lifetime relationship not a four-year relationship. And what Kim Mulkey did for Baylor that year was a blessing from heaven," says former Baylor basketball coach Carroll Dawson, now an executive with the NBA Houston Rockets and the WNBA Houston Comets. He was the head coach at Baylor for four years in the 1970s.

"We needed something that season to be positive and that team did that. She did that," Dawson says. "The previous year, we were in the news for all the wrong reasons. Now we were in the news for all the right reasons and we had Kim to thank for that."

11

That Championship Season

When I look back, I think our championship season actually began the previous year when we lost in the Sweet 16 to Tennessee in such heartbreaking fashion. Many times I have been asked if that game had an impact on our program and me. It did. We were not about to forget what happened. I would be at my children's games that summer and I would still be thinking about it. It was hard to let go.

When the players gathered the next summer to start training for the following season, each player was given a T-shirt that read "00:02." We wrote "2-10ths" on our locker room board and it stayed there all season. We saw it every day. It was just so gut wrenching. We never talked about it—and we didn't have to. Experiencing it made us a better team. I wouldn't say it was *the* motivating factor for us, but it certainly was *a* motivating factor. We learned from that game. We learned how to finish games. I think that situation helped our team prepare for the next season. The feeling was, "I want to get over *that.*" Make no mistake, though. We did not let ourselves forget.

You never know which year is going to be The Year. You hope for it every year, but as a coach, you can't allow yourself to think along those lines. You have to think smaller—the next practice, the next game. I knew we had a good team. We had unbelievable chemistry. We had great leadership from the seniors. They went through a lot. I never—not once—had to deal with any issues from my players that season. There were no problems with discipline, academics, missed classes, playing time, playing a certain role, or anything else. There were no incidents. The older players were mature beyond their years and they led the younger players. It felt like I was coaching a team of grown women that season. It was such a great pleasure to get up every morning and go to work. It's rare that you have a season like that.

We had three seniors on the team and one of them, Melanie Hammerly, rarely played. I am so proud of Melanie, who is now coaching at Waco High School. She epitomized what I meant by every player on our team understanding her role. Melanie accepted her role and played hard every day in practice regardless of how much playing time she got in the games. Every day she was one of the first players on the floor. She was, after all, a coach's daughter. Her mother not only coached basketball but also volleyball and track. Melanie had played high school basketball in Orange, Texas. She was 6 feet 5 inches tall and could alter shots. She was also a terrific volleyball player. In fact, after her basketball eligibility expired, she played volleyball at Baylor for a season. Out of all the players on the team, I think Melanie grew the most spiritually and personally.

We also had the Blackmon twins, Steffanie and Tiffanie. We signed them out of Rowlett High School in the Dallas area. They were crucial to building our program, even though by the time she was a senior, Tiffanie was injured and unable to play. Tiffanie continued as a student coach for the team and took her role very seriously.

Steffanie ended up being our starting center. She and Sophia Young worked terrificly in tandem despite their completely opposite personalities. Steffanie was very quiet, a perfectionist who studied scouting reports thoroughly and was a wiz in the classroom. She became the program's first academic All-American. Sophia was more outgoing, more approachable. With her everything didn't have to always be perfect. Steffanie was injured at the tail end of the previous season, hurting her knee in the Big 12 Tournament. She rehabbed her knee and had a great senior year. Not only did she help us win a National Championship, but she shared co-MVP honors with Sophia Young at our team banquet.

We opened the season against LSU, which had the best player in the country, Seimone Augustus; one of the best point guards, Temeka Johnson; and one of the best young post players, Sylvia Fowles. LSU went to the Final Four the year before, was ranked No. 3 in the country going into the game, and was definitely a force to be reckoned with. We, on the other hand, were ranked No. 8.

The game was at a neutral site, Austin, Texas. We fell behind by 21 points and I wondered if we had the kind of team that could come back. I took a timeout. I told the players we were going to be all right, but I kept thinking this was our first game and we were down by so many points to a good team. It would be very easy for us to lose our focus and get blown out. We didn't.

I have never had a team quit on me and it wasn't about to start with this game. Our players kept competing and we came back and had a chance at the end to win the game. We had the ball for the last shot. We didn't execute the play, but after that game I remember thinking that one day we would execute at the end of the game and win. This was just the first game.

Although it was our first game, I saw enough to confirm what I thought before the season started: We were going to be pretty darn good. LSU was one of the top teams in the country and we held our own against them. I was confident we could compete for the Big 12 title, but would we be good enough to make it to the Final Four? As the season went on, I became more and more confident that we would. We just kept getting better and better.

The first big thing we did was win the regular season Big 12 Championship. That's what you play for. The regular season championship means so much more to me than the tournament championship. Any team can get hot in three games on a neutral court and win the tournament. I believe that winning the regular season championship by playing 16 games against your conference opponents both home and away is much more of an accomplishment.

As the season progressed, the biggest difference I saw in the team was that we were able to win the close games that we hadn't won the previous year. We learned how to compete and how to win. When you do that, championships start to come. We beat No. 7 ranked Texas by three points. We lost a triple-overtime game to Nebraska in Lincoln where we shot 21 fewer free throws. We won two close games against Texas Tech who was ranked No. 12. We beat Oklahoma on the road by one point. These were all games that showed how much better we were than the year before.

The Big 12 championship game was also important to me in an entirely different way. I am a private person, especially when it comes to health issues. I only allow a certain number of people into my inner circle. That's partly my personality and partly because of what I do for a living. In this business you can't get too close to people. I have found that my life really doesn't have much privacy, regardless of how private I would like it to be.

I am very open professionally and answer almost any question a member of the media asks. Reporters appreciate my candor and honesty, but at the same time, I don't feel that my personal issues should be made public. To me, you just don't go there. The administrators at

Baylor sometimes think I am accessible almost to a fault, but I want to help get the Lady Bears exposure in any way that I can.

On the day we won the regular season Big 12 championship, I had a breast biopsy. There's breast cancer in my family—both my maternal grandmother and my mother are survivors. Their cancer was found in the early stages, so they're both fine. My grandmother had a mastectomy and my mother had a lumpectomy. I am not a hypochondriac and I rarely get sick, but I am also smart enough to know that I need to have a PAP smear and mammogram every year. I also know that because of my family history, I am at high risk.

Visible on my mammogram was a little spot. I saw a vascular surgeon on the morning we played Texas Tech for the conference championship. He did an ultrasound and determined that it was only an abnormal looking cyst. He withdrew fluid from the cyst and the surgeon immediately knew that it was benign. He didn't even have to send the sample off to have it tested. No one ever knew about it. We won the championship and I never thought about it again. I still have to remind myself that my grandmother and my mother are both survivors. I'm well aware of what the statistics say—next in line is yours truly.

We won the Big 12 tournament that season in Kansas City, beating Kansas State in the championship game. We were given a No. 2 seed in the NCAA Tournament and were sent to Seattle for the first two games.

Before we left for Seattle, I saw the same surgeon, Dr. David Hoffman, for something quite different and, as it turned out, something more serious. I was attending my son's basketball game and sitting in the stands with my primary care physician. I mentioned to him that I was having pain and swelling in my abdomen. He had me come in for a visit, did a workup, and ordered a CT scan. The scan showed something very suspicious and the doctors thought I might have an internal hernia.

Basically, as it was explained to me, the intestines do not form the way they are supposed to *in utero*. There are no outward signs of it at birth and doctors would not suspect it. I told the doctors who examined me that for as long as I could remember, I had abdominal pain on and off. It always went away, however, so it wasn't something I constantly worried about. I was told that such a hernia was very uncommon but when it does occur, it usually leads to a bowel obstruction. I had a tender spot near my naval that hurt when touched. This symptom bothered me the most.

Dr. Hoffman wanted to immediately operate on an outpatient basis, but we were getting ready to leave for Seattle and I simply did not have the time. I agreed to go to the hospital in Seattle if I felt any pain that lasted for an extended period of time. Right before our game against Oregon, I had to find a room to lie down in at the gym. The pain was so severe that I needed peace and quiet and a place to relax. Approximately 10 to 15 minutes before the start of the game, I began to feel better. I was able to make it all the way through the NCAA Tournament and attend the many post-tournament celebrations before I had the surgery. Dr. Hoffman did the procedure in an hour, and pretty soon after that, I was back to my normal routine, which consists of a lot of running and abdominal crunches. He actually removed a lot of scar tissue but didn't find the suspected hernia. Who knew that I had so much scar tissue? I have never been in an accident or had surgery.

When I was younger, I hated to jog. Now, I try to jog for 30 minutes a day on a treadmill. I do it Monday through Friday and take the weekends off. Before I jog, I do some stretching exercises and about 75 crunches. For the first 15 minutes of my run, I carry one-pound weights in each hand. I never imagined doing all of this, but once I had children, I said to myself, "Whoa, you gotta do something here, girl!" I'm not interested in getting a certain time or competing in a marathon—I exercise so I can eat!

After Seattle, we moved on to beat Minnesota and advance to the Elite Eight for the first time in Baylor's history. We upset North Carolina, the top seed in our region, to make it to the Final Four. In that game, Chelsea Whitaker, our point guard, did an exceptional job guarding Ivory Latta, who was an All-American.

Chelsea, who was also a senior, knew how to compete. She didn't have the greatest shot in the world and there were times when I had to remind her that we didn't need her to throw the ball into the first row of seats, but she had an undeniable presence on the floor. As our point guard, I was on her all the time to run our offense as efficiently as she could.

Chelsea made some big plays for us and hit some big shots for us, too. If you challenged her to shoot the ball, she didn't hesitate. Iowa State did that to her and she scored 20 points against them. She also hit a last second lay-up to beat Texas Tech in the Big 12 tournament.

When we got to Indianapolis, everything that happened was incredibly emotional and exciting. There was so much to do. I don't know if my having been there before as a player and an assistant coach helped, but I like to think it did.

We played Louisiana State in the first semifinal game, a rematch of the first game of the season. They were 33–2 and ranked No. 2 in the country. What I remember about the LSU game was falling behind, again, this time by a 24–9 score with 7:30 left in the first half. We were shooting horribly and we had a ton of turnovers. LSU was killing us in transition because we were having trouble getting our defense set up. I called a time out and told my assistants that we were getting embarrassed on national television. In the huddle, I reminded the kids that we had been down to this team before and fought back. I told them to relax. This was the Final Four and it was understandable if they were nervous, but they needed to settle down.

I knew we needed to get Sophia more involved. I decided to use a zone defense, which I almost never do. As a player, I played man-to-man defense. I coach man-to-man defense but sometimes you have to do whatever it takes to win. We needed to try something different.

We scored the last eight points of the half and that was good enough to tie the game. Our team was fired up, all the players ran into the locker room. During the break, I emphasized how poorly we had played even though we were tied. I talked about strategy, about how we were going to continue to play the 3–2 zone defense, and what areas we needed to guard. We kept it going in the second half and won by 11 points.

Chameka Scott started in the backcourt with Chelsea Whitaker. Chameka was one of the most articulate and intelligent players I've ever coached. She hit a big three-pointer in the LSU game to start our comeback. There was a Louisiana Tech connection to Chameka as well. Her high school coach in Texas was Pam Crawford, who was a teammate of mine on the 1983–84 Lady Techsters team. Chameka paid her dues at Baylor. She didn't play very much as a freshman, but by the time we reached the Final Four, she was a regular starter. She was an excellent rebounder for her size and I always tried to assign her to guard the best player on the other team. Chameka had a very outgoing, infectious personality—finding time for everybody and anybody. She was a big fan favorite.

Jordan Davis was another important player on the team as much for what she did on the bench as on the court. Jordan remains one of the best team players I have ever coached. She was an excellent shooter and was always the first one on the bench to wave a towel or congratulate the players on the floor. She was one of the three captains of the team in 2005–06. Although she only averaged seven minutes a game for us that year, it was a miracle that she was even able to do that!

What made Jordan's situation so remarkable was that she survived a blood clot passing through her heart. I noticed during our preseason workouts before her junior year that she couldn't finish drills, she looked winded, and she was always gasping for air. No one could find anything wrong, but after seeing this for about two or three weeks, I finally told her and our trainer, "Don't come back tomorrow unless you've got a doctor with you." Finally, after seeing a number of specialists, they found a clot and determined that it had passed through her heart and she was lucky to be alive. She sat out her junior season, 2003–04, as a medical red-shirt and returned to the team the following year.

I only used eight players in the LSU game including reserves: Emily Niemann, Latoya Wyatt, and Angela Tisdale. Latoya was a sophomore, although she had played at the local community college before coming to Baylor. She played an extremely important role for us that year, especially in the NCAA Tournament where she made a lot of big shots. Unfortunately, her playing time decreased over the next two years due in part to injuries. We just couldn't keep her healthy. Nevertheless, I knew how valuable she was the year we won it all.

Angela Tisdale was a freshman the year we won the championship. She was from Austin and she backed up Chelsea. Angela has taken the brunt of my coaching over the years, because as a former point guard, I am the toughest on point guards. She is the best shooting point guard I have ever coached and, over the years, she has learned to be more outspoken. You can't play point guard for me if you don't open your mouth! You've got to be in charge on the floor.

Emily Niemann was a sophomore and came from an athletic family in Houston. She was a fabulous outside shooter which for her size, 6 feet 1 inches tall, made her a very tough player to guard.

After our win over LSU everyone thought we would have a rematch against Tennessee, who was playing Michigan State in the other semifinal. Tennessee had beaten LSU in the Southeastern Conference tournament championship just prior to the NCAA Tournament and was loaded. However, Michigan State won with a big comeback in the second half, which meant that the championship win would be a first ever for either college.

The night we played Michigan State for the NCAA Championship, I walked into the RCA Dome and saw two men with a sign: "Here's To You, Mulkey-Robertson, Jesus Loves You More Than You Will Know." Well, I don't think those guys knew that *The Graduate* is one of my all-time favorite movies or how much I love the Simon & Garfunkel soundtrack from that movie. I took it to be a good omen.

In the championship game we trailed only once, 2–0. We had a 19-point lead with 3:13 left in the first half, but by halftime it was cut to 12. That didn't sit well with me, so when I talked to the team, I challenged them. We got the lead back to 19 points midway through the second half and never let up. Afterward, I was told that the margin of victory—22 points—was the second largest in the history of the NCAA Women's championship game. Unfortunately, I remember quite well the most lopsided score, 67–44. I was on the losing end of that one, as an assistant coach at Louisiana Tech. Tennessee won that game.

I wore a powder-blue outfit for the championship game. That's Louisiana Tech's color but that's not why I wore it. My assistant found the outfit and wanted me to wear it. Needless to say, I am never, ever going to wear it again. It's on a hanger in my closet at home, still dirty—stains and all.

When I think back and remember how we got to that point, the places we played in, the teams we had to play, and the No. 1 seeds we had to beat; it was a remarkable journey. We didn't have the luxury of playing at home during the NCAA Tournament. We weren't even close to home. It makes it even sweeter to think that we didn't have any advantages along the way. We went out there and we earned it.

The championship was huge for Baylor University and the city of Waco. I don't think any of us realized just how huge it was until we returned from Indianapolis. We knew there were supposed to be some fans waiting at Baylor to greet us. What we didn't know, or expect, was that the Ferrell Center would be filled with screaming and excited fans. Clips from the National Championship game were playing on the video boards and the arena was overflowing with fans standing on their feet. It was as if we had won the championship all over again—everyone was just going wild. Later there was a parade through downtown Waco. I doubt any of us will forget riding in Corvette convertibles and the sight, when our cars topped the hill, of the throng of people cheering on the sides of the street below us. The parade was held two weeks after we won the championship, yet people were still incredibly excited.

People in the community would come up to me and ask, "Do you really understand how big this is? Do you?" I don't know if I did then, but I do now. What I don't understand, what I can't understand, is what it meant to those diehard Baylor fans that have been fans for 30 or 40 years. I had only been at Baylor for five years. One woman told me, "All we've ever known, Coach, is wait until next year." That just really hit me. It was such a joy watching the community and the players revel in the victory.

Our office was flooded with congratulatory letters and emails. We got one from two longtime UConn fans who wrote, "Your team won our hearts in the early rounds of the NCAA and we must tell you that it was easy to be a Baylor fan for a couple of weeks." Football coaches from the Big 12 Conference sent notes and Carroll Dawson sent flowers. A story editor for a literary agency in California sent me a letter after reading about my situation at Louisiana Tech. "Celebrate long and hard," she wrote. "And I hope in some private moment you were able to dance on your court, take pride in a job not only well done, but done with dignity—and know that all those who doubted you now know how wrong they were. Thank you for being such an inspiration."

I received many phone calls after winning the championship. One call in particular stands out in my mind. A few months after we won the telephone rang in the basketball office. At that time, I was sitting at my administrative assistant's desk and answered the phone myself. This voice said, "Coach, can you hold for Bob Knight." I was thinking to myself, "It's not really going to be Bob Knight." Nevertheless, I stayed on hold and stayed on hold until he finally came on the line. I was honored and soaked up every bit of wisdom this basketball great offered. He told me that I might have better teams, but I might not ever win another National Championship so I should enjoy this one. He also said that I should never let anyone else's expectations affect my players or me. No one knows the team better than the coach does.

Regardless of how one feels about Bob Knight, the man is a great coach, especially when it comes to making players exceed expectations. He didn't have to make that phone call to me, but he did. When you are in this profession and you get a call from someone of Bob Knight's stature you never forget it—and I won't.

Among the many fun and eventful things that happened to me and the team after we won the title was going to New York City to receive the Winged Foot Award, which is given to the coaches of the men's and women's NCAA championship teams. Roy Williams of North Carolina was there to receive the men's award. The team was honored at the state capital in Austin and at the White House. As you can imagine, it's not every day that you get to meet the president. These kinds of things come with winning a championship. I think we met every politician in Texas and Washington, DC. There have been so many events and so many memories. The parade in Waco and the reception at the Ferrell Center are two of my fondest. You need to enjoy a win like that while it lasts. I think all of the players will tell you the same thing—we enjoyed every moment.

That year our team was nominated for an ESPY Award. I took Makenzie to California where the awards ceremony was being held. We didn't win, but it was still an exciting time.

One morning while we were in Los Angeles I woke up very early to work out on the treadmill in the hotel's exercise room. It was 6:00 AM and I never thought anyone would be in the room at such an early hour. I was wrong.

When I opened the door, I noticed a man on one of the treadmills. The room had only two treadmills, one right next to the other. As I got closer, I recognized the man. It was Bill Belichick, the coach of the New England Patriots. I obviously knew who he was. I had followed his career, but I doubted he had a clue who I was. I introduced myself and, for the next hour and a half, we had a great conversation. Although he was walking because of a leg injury, I was jogging the whole time. I have never in my life jogged for that long on a treadmill. I just kept going and going.

We were two strangers who didn't know each other, but because of the coaching profession, we had a common bond and interest. We talked as if we were long lost friends. The memory of that morning, the things we talked about—from our children and the nature of athletics, to the difference between professional sports and college sports—is one I will never forget.

A couple of weeks later a box arrived at my home and inside was New England Patriots gear, a gift from Bill. He later sent me an autographed copy of his book, *The Education of a Coach*, and as I read it, I could certainly identify with the parts relating to how the coaching profession affects your spouse and impacts your home life.

There was no honor or award that touched me more than a note I received from one of my former players at Louisiana Tech, Erica Westbrooks. She was the Most Outstanding Player of the 1988 Final Four, the last time Louisiana Tech won the national championship. She wrote, "This is for all you taught me and more. I am so proud you got your chance and you made the best of it. Please continue at Baylor—I have two daughters who are going to be tall. You are still very much in my mind and a very important part of my life."

I remember being asked before the Final Four what it was like to be playing against LSU, given that I was from Louisiana and had even been recruited to play there. I told the reporter that the only thing that bothered me about having to play LSU was that they were going home after the Final Four to eat crawfish and I was not. I added that some of my folks from back home would be in Waco in a few weeks with lots of crawfish to satisfy my appetite.

That's exactly what happened, too. Every spring at the end of the Baylor basketball season one of the first telephone calls I make is to Tom Parent in Natalbany, Louisiana. I used to play football with his sons and our families had barbecues together when I was a kid. My mom still calls him if she needs any repair work done on her home.

Tom puts together a crawfish boil for me at my home in Waco. Tom's brother, Paul, comes down from North Carolina in his motor home and stops in Louisiana. The two of them, along with their wives, get 300 pounds of crawfish, 60 crabs, and 50 pounds of jumbo shrimp and put them all on ice. They leave Louisiana on a Friday morning and arrive in Waco about 10 hours later. My mother and some other relatives make the trip as well.

The Parents put the water on to boil early Saturday morning and do up all their seasonings—onions, garlic, and a whole bunch of good stuff—and prepare the ingredients that go into the water. Everything is ready to eat by the afternoon. Some years we've had as many as 75 people at our house. My assistant coaches come. Some of the faculty comes. The parents of my children's friends come. The whole thing lasts well into the night and it's not too often that there is much left to eat the next morning.

It's the ideal way to end the season and it was especially sweet after the championship season.

12

Departures

For many years now going to the Florida beaches is one of my favorite vacation trips. That was true when I was in college and it was true in the summer of 2005, months after we won the championship. My family usually rents a condominium in Destin, Florida, which is on the Gulf Coast, some 30 miles east of Pensacola. We generally go there in August, right after the July recruiting season has concluded, to get some downtime before the next season begins. After everything we had done, and everywhere we had gone following our 2005 championship, I was looking forward to this little respite more than I had any other year.

On August 2, I received a message on my cell phone from Emily Niemann asking that I give her a call. Emily had just finished her sophomore year at Baylor and was one of the key players on the championship team. I was looking forward to having her back. Emily's message said that she and her dad needed to talk to me. Before I could call her back, though, she left another message on my phone. This one said that I didn't need to return her call because she had sent me an email instead.

I was on vacation and didn't travel with a computer, but my assistant, Johnny Derrick, had his laptop with him. When I read what she had written the first thought that came to mind was that she was playing a joke on me. The note said she was unhappy at Baylor and wanted to transfer. Honestly, I thought I was *Punk'd*. (That is the name of the former television show on MTV where pranks were played on celebrities—a 21st-century version of *Candid Camera*.) The show was popular with the players and the thought that she was playing a joke on me made more sense than what she had written in her email.

I waited a few minutes because I thought for sure another email would show up in my mailbox. When nothing arrived I picked up the phone and called her. For the next 45 minutes I talked to her and her father, listening to the reasons she gave for wanting to leave. I was shocked, angry, and disappointed. But at no time during the conversation did I ever feel that any of the reasons she was giving me were really the reasons why she was leaving. I just didn't believe her.

Emily Niemann came to Baylor from the Westbury Christian School in Houston and was named the state's Private School Player of the Year in 2003. She was recruited by several Big 12 Conference teams but ended up attending Baylor because, as she explained it then, "God wants me at Baylor." Now two years later she was telling her coach that she wanted to leave.

It wasn't just a shock. It was an earthquake to me and to the whole program. Emily played a significant role on our team and I was expecting big things from her. She had a terrific game against Michigan State in the championship game, changing the whole complexion by making some big three-pointers. That was her specialty.

I don't make this statement lightly: Emily Niemann was the best shooter I have ever coached. I spent 19 years of my life at Louisiana Tech with some of the greatest players to ever play the game, but Emily's range, for a six-foot one-inch post player, was unbelievable. Her accuracy was unbelievable. When she missed a shot, we were always surprised and even a bit disappointed. We naturally believed that she was going to make every shot, every time. It was the equivalent of watching Tiger Woods make a big putt. You just knew he was going to make it. The same was true for Emily.

Although she was limited in some areas, I loved Emily's game. She was not the fastest or the strongest. She didn't jump the highest. Nevertheless, she knew how to compete. I always compared her to Larry Bird.

When a player transfers a coach can usually see it coming. But I never saw this one coming. I was blind-sided. Players transfer all the time for any number of reasons, from conflicts with coaches to disputes over playing time. Coaches are human. We'd love all of the players we recruit to stay with us, but we understand that isn't the case in this business. There isn't a single program that can say every player it recruits leaves as a happy individual.

As a coach you understand that these things happen. You don't expect all the players you coach to understand or even like everything you do on the court. In the recruiting process, I tell players upfront what they can expect from me. I want them to exceed what they think they are physically capable of doing on the basketball court. As coaches we will take care of their health and safety and any injuries. That is our obligation as adults and professionals. I also want them to earn a degree. The only way they're not going to get a degree is if they don't go to class—and they are not going to be in our program if they don't go to class.

I am not going to take it personally if after a player graduates she says some negative things about the basketball program or about me. It's disappointing, but I feel that if a player doesn't recognize the value of her experience at that time, then later, and it may be 15 or 20 years later, she will understand what we were trying to do.

We had no choice but to release a statement that announced that Emily wanted to transfer and was requesting a release. Before I would give her the release, however, I wanted to know the real reason why she was leaving, and I wanted to hear it from her face-to-face. I chose to cut short my vacation. I could have stayed and delayed dealing with the issue, but I knew something wasn't adding up. It was bizarre! Looking back now, I wish I had stayed on vacation and dealt with it after I was done relaxing with my family.

We arranged a meeting in Waco with Emily, her parents Steve and Kelly Niemann, the athletic director, Ian McCaw, and the school's interim president, Bill Underwood. Normally, you would not need to have all these people in the same room for a meeting like this, but this was such an unusual set of circumstances. I wanted somebody there who would be as objective as possible and would tell me what he or she thought was really going on. There were many, many reasons Emily gave for wanting to leave, but I will never believe those were her reasons for leaving a National Championship team. They were all basketball related. She wondered if she'd be a starter. She didn't like it when I substituted for her on the defensive end. She wanted to be known as more than a three-point shooter. I was too hard on some of the other players. I had an answer for every reason and that's why I suspected that there was something else behind her decision.

We spent several hours talking and listening to Emily until I decided to give her the release. She was granted what is termed a partial release, meaning she would be allowed to contact schools that were approved in advance by Baylor, schools that did not play in the Big 12 Conference, and schools that did not appear on future Lady Bears' playing schedule. She ended up transferring to the University of California at Santa Barbara where she was required by the NCAA transfer rules to sit out the 2005–06 season.

To this day, my opinion is that Emily was not unhappy with me, the coaches, or the university. I believe unhappiness comes from within one's soul. I believe coaches can frustrate and anger a player. I believe they can do things that a player doesn't understand or agree with, but one's unhappiness comes from within.

At the end of the 2005–06 season Emily decided to leave California-Santa Barbara. I said to myself, "Isn't life interesting?" When we recruited her, and while she was at Baylor, all Emily ever said was that she wanted a shot at the WNBA; she couldn't live without basketball. I will always worry about Emily. I will always care about Emily.

I beat myself up over her departure. I asked myself, "What could I have done differently?" In time, I came to the realization that nothing we did as a staff was wrong. I couldn't dwell on it any longer; it was time to move forward.

In February 2007, *USA Today* came out with a story about Emily Niemann. She was attending the University of Massachusetts and was married to Ashley Taylor, a woman she met at Baylor. The two women had chosen a new surname, Nkosi. Massachusetts is the only state where gay marriage is legal and this was the first time that Niemann publicly revealed that she was a lesbian. In the article,

Niemann said she feared she would lose her scholarship had her sexual orientation become public, something Baylor strongly denies.

❧

Later that same month, Hurricane Katrina hit New Orleans and southern Louisiana. My mother and grandmother live 40 miles north of the city and I was understandably quite concerned. My mother's home in Hammond was without power for a couple of weeks, but my sister was able to help. Things could have been much worse. Hurricane Rita followed closely on the heels of Katrina and this time my sister's home was in the storm's path and badly damaged. It took her and her family more than a year to get their situation resolved. I was thinking, what else could possibly go wrong? One of my best players transfers. Two hurricanes hit Louisiana. Little did I know what was to come.

Marriage is a commitment between two people—a binding agreement "'til death do us part." I was an adult when my parents divorced and yet the effects were devastating. Anyone who has known me for any period of time knows how I feel about divorce. They also know how important my family is to me.

I am not exaggerating by any means when I say that I felt like the bottom fell out from my world when Randy told me that he was no longer happy in our marriage. I was floored. Surely any problems we had were no greater than those of other married couples with children and careers. How could he just walk away from our marriage, our children, and our family?

It was a long, hard summer with no real vacation break. I couldn't fathom what was happening. I was again in a situation where I didn't feel like I was seeing the whole picture or getting all the facts. You don't just leave your marriage without direction or somewhere to go. I will never forget my mother coming into my room one evening. She hugged me and the kids and said, "A man does not leave a beautiful family like this unless he has a plan. One of these days you will learn what that plan is. Sit back and the truth will fall in your lap." She felt that there had to be something or someone to encourage him to do what he did. Otherwise, it made no sense. Her words did not mean a lot to me at the time, but they did stay with me.

For months I fought and struggled to find a solution. I tried to make sense of Randy's actions. He blamed me and I blamed myself. I was on a daily roller coaster of emotions. I searched for reasons, always giving him the benefit of the doubt. I thought he was going through a mid-life crisis or an identity crisis. I was concerned that he might be feeling secondary to my career, as so often happens in the coaching field. I searched for ways to convince him otherwise.

After 18 years of marriage and 23 years together as a couple, our lives had settled into a routine just like a lot of other marriages. I felt our problems were the problems connected to the normal life cycle of a married couple. I understood and recognized that along the way, especially once you have children and become more involved in their activities, it becomes very easy to neglect each other.

I never wanted a divorce and I told Randy when he walked out the door that he better be sure because there was no turning back. This was not going to be "break up" and "make up" like high school kids.

Although too late, we attended marriage counseling. The counselor agreed that the problems Randy and I were facing were no different from those of many couples and they certainly were not worth the dissolution of our marriage. Randy still filed for divorce.

I know there is no perfect marriage. But I really believed we had a very good marriage. Randy's business was doing very well and the kids were really happy with their schools and friends. Waco was fast beginning to feel like home for all of us.

Randy expressed to me on several occasions that he felt neglected but never did I think he was talking about something that would lead to divorce. My first inkling that he was seriously considering divorce came when were driving back to Waco after a Dallas Cowboys football game just before the beginning of the 2005–06 season.

I recognized early on that Randy saw a different type of lifestyle in Waco than I did, one that he was particularly drawn to. There was much more of a social life available to both of us as well as the opportunity for him to earn more money. I was content to coach and do what I had always done—spend time with family and follow the children's sporting activities. My relaxation is and always was attending their practices and games. I truly enjoy sitting in the car and watching them practice, just as my grandmother did for me when I went roller skating as a child.

Randy quickly became attached to the social scene, enjoying the many opportunities to mix and mingle with other couples. In our early years of dating and marriage in Louisiana, we lived the small-town life. That was an ideal pace and setting for me. I loved it. I am a small-town girl and even little Ruston represented big-city life. Randy, on the other hand, lived in larger cities around the country while growing up. The move to Waco was tempting to him in many ways.

At one point during the counseling sessions, I offered to quit my job at Baylor so I could devote all of my attention to my husband and to the rebuilding of our marriage. I have always said that my family comes first and this was a prime example of what I meant. The value of my marriage and family far outweighed the value of my career. I knew everyone in our family benefited from and enjoyed the perks that came with my collegiate coaching success, but I was more than willing to set that aside to save my marriage. It was a sacrifice I was willing to make, but it was not a viable solution to Randy. I had a sense that there was more to it than some desire to seek happiness.

Divorce does not only affect a husband and a wife. Its ugly tentacles have far-reaching effects. Immediate families are torn apart, extended families are hurt, friendships dissolve, and those close to the couple are forced to choose sides. I still find it difficult to say "my divorce." The whole idea is such a foreign concept to me. I don't know when that will change. I can say it. I am living it. But there are times when it still hits me—I'm divorced.

Nothing is ever the same again. Happiness is really a temporary state. The path he chose to find his happiness left a wake of destruction. I still held out hope that the counselor, a neutral party, would reach Randy in some way. The counselor met with us together and individually. His encouragement and advice was for us to stay married and to commit to working out our problems especially for the sake of our children who were 14 and 11 at the time. However, after a one-on-one session with the counselor, I left with the realization that the desire for a divorce was "about Randy."

Finally after several counseling sessions, Randy and I met at a local restaurant and he told me that it was over. It was two days before Christmas. He wanted to wait until after the holidays to tell the children and hoped we could tell them together. As I was heading home, I knew I was not going to be able to hold my emotions for that long. I went straight to my bedroom while my mother entertained the children and friends who were at our house. Finally, Kramer sensed that something was wrong, and when he asked me, I couldn't hold it in any longer. It was excruciating. A little more than two weeks later, after a home game against Texas, Randy waited for us at our house. That's when he told them he was leaving.

My divorce has caused me a great deal of pain. The greatest hurt I have experienced is that of a mother watching her children cope with the complexities of a family torn apart. Nonetheless, it is amazing to see how they deal with it in their own way. Thank goodness they were born with self-confidence and learned right from wrong. The divorce hurts them so much because they were raised to believe that you don't divorce; it is wrong. I tell them, "Love your daddy. He needs you. You need your daddy. But, walking out that door is wrong and don't ever think that it's right." I won't ever change my view of that.

They were wounded, but they never used the situation as an excuse for anything. Their grades never dropped. They didn't go through a depression or exhibit any emotional changes. They continued to participate in their sports and activities with friends just as they always did. I am inspired by their childlike ability to move forward with their lives and not dwell on what is no longer. They are little champions.

I am not going to pretend and play nice about the divorce. That's not me. If anything, for the sake of my children, I have to continue to be the same person I have always been. Some people may not agree with my approach, but when all is said and done, my kids will know that I was upfront and honest with them. They know they can count on me to be the same person I've always been. They also know they are loved.

I discovered my most fragile moments throughout the ordeal, and just when I might have been at a breaking point, the thought of my children gave me an overwhelming boost of strength. They are moving forward with their lives and I am moving forward with mine, too. I've been through all the stages—denial, anger, hurt, anger, disbelief, anger—did I say anger? The divorce was, and remains, a very unpleasant part of my life. I don't choose to dwell on it because he still lives in Waco. But it seems like every day I'm hit with it again. Of all the enticements that I may encounter to leave Baylor and Waco, I don't think there is any salary, facility, administration, or anything else that would give me a better reason than to not have to deal with Randy on a daily basis. I do not understand how he walked away from our family and thought that I was still going to want to be his friend afterward. What in my past would make him or anyone else think that?

In the end, he put a dollar value on our life together. That was just another blow to me. Not the money so much as the discovery that the man I was married to for so long just wanted freedom and money to pursue his happiness. He held out his hand and I wrote a check. He could have taken more of my money than he did. The law allowed him half of everything. Because he didn't, I agreed that he did not have to pay child support. The only money he is required to pay is half of the uninsured medical expenses for the children that my insurance does not cover.

I still don't understand how Randy could simply walk away from his family. But I am no longer in turmoil. I have moved on with my life.

13

Moving Forward

There are times when God truly does work in myste-rious ways. In the same month that Randy first men-tioned that he thought our marriage was in trouble, one of my dear friends from Hammond, Ralph Gaude, passed away. Ralph and his wife, Cheryl Gaude, had been my close friends since I was in high school. Ralph suffered a broken neck in an automobile accident and was left a quadriplegic. He was training to be a military air traffic controller at the time of the accident and most of his unit eventually deployed to Vietnam.

When I was in high school, I often rode to away games with the Gaudes, sitting in the front seat while Ralph drove his specially equipped van. Occasionally, some teammates would come along as well. (You could do that back then. These days, you must ride with the team on the bus.)

My letter of intent to attend Louisiana Tech was even signed at the Gaudes' house mainly because it was only a few blocks from the high school and there was more room to accommodate all the people who were attending. Cheryl was always one of my biggest fans. She kept my high school scorebook all four years that I played, and when I went to college, Ralph and Cheryl drove to my home games my freshman year. Dr. Taylor even had a ramp built to allow Ralph's wheelchair access to Memorial Gym. They stopped coming after my first year, but I didn't find out why until much later. Ralph, like my father, did not appreciate the way Coach Barmore was using me in my role off the bench for the Lady Techsters.

When Ralph passed away from a heart attack, I flew back to Hammond to deliver a eulogy at his funeral service. A few months later, Cheryl came to visit us in Waco. She wanted to spend some time with us and watch the Lady Bears play. What started out as a visit evolved into a situation where we both realized that she was supposed to be with us at that particular time. She filled a void in our lives and I felt that we were doing the same in hers. She ended up staying with us, helping with the kids, and above all, helping me. She was and still is a godsend.

I think it was good for Cheryl and it helped her in the grieving process, but it has also been good for me in my own grieving process. She has two homes now—one in Hammond and ours in Waco. She stays with us because she feels needed, wanted, and loved. We're not going to let her leave us just yet. She's a part of our family.

I told everyone who asked that I didn't think of the 2005–06 season as a season in which we were defending the championship. That sounds like somebody is going to take the championship away and no one will ever do that. The banner will always hang in the Ferrell Center. Instead, we decided to approach the season the same way as every other coach and team in America: it was a new season and we would like to do the same thing we did last year. I'm sure Geno Auriemma said the same thing to his Connecticut teams after his championships and I'm sure Pat Summitt said the same thing to her Tennessee team before the start of the 2007–08 season.

We were not the same basketball team, however. We had lost seven players on the team, but we still had a great nucleus of players, with three starters returning. However, we also had a group of freshmen eager to learn and find their places. It was a totally different team and I felt that we had to find our identity as well as our strengths and weaknesses.

There was no denying one thing: The championship made us a program that was respected in the Big 12 Conference and around the country. When I visit a recruit now, I can tell her how quickly we won a National Championship and that we have many more left in us, so she should come help us win another. That's exciting. I look back on what Coach Bob Knight told me and he's right. I may never win another championship and there are so many excellent coaches who never even win one. But having won one has brought respectability to the program. A great feeling—that's what a championship gives you. It is something to be proud of. It makes me the most proud to see the respect that the Lady Bears have around the country. Tom Stanton and I talked about that when he hired me. He wanted to bring a higher level of respect and integrity to the athletic programs at Baylor. That was the same thing that Ian McCaw said when he signed me to my latest extension. None of this could have happened without the support from the athletic administration and the university. It all starts at the top.

Baylor is now on the women's basketball map and in the mix for the better players. We can look at McDonald's All-Americans, and more importantly, they can look at us. That's not to say we can rest on our laurels. We can't— and we won't. But it's exciting to see the transformation of the program.

I can remember when Chelsea Whitaker was a senior at Skyline High School in Dallas. It was 2000, my first year at Baylor. Chelsea never even gave Baylor a thought even though we are only 90 minutes away from Dallas. We never gave Chelsea a thought either. She was precisely the kind of player—All-State, honorable mention All-American—that we didn't recruit at that time because, frankly, it would have been a waste of our time to try. She ended up going to the University of Virginia. After one season there she hurt her knee, and while she was recuperating, she saw what was happening at Baylor. She saw a winning program with winning players like Sheila

Lambert and Danielle Crockrom. She transferred to Baylor, played three years for us, and ended up being the starting point guard on our National Championship team her senior year. I know it sounds trite, but it is amazing what winning can do.

Before the start of the 2005–06 season, I received an award that touched me as much or more than any other. It was a community service award for "bridging the gap" between Baylor University and the African American community in Waco. Several local pastors from the African American community presented the university with a grandfather clock that stands in the reception area to the basketball office. I have a miniature replica that sits on my office desk.

I try to be active in the community. I speak at clubs and schools. During the season, my children and I are involved in the local Meals on Wheels program. The community, in kind, has embraced the Lady Bears.

We started a welcome back potluck supper when I arrived at Baylor. It was originally held in a room in the school's business center and maybe 120 people would come. Now, we hold it at the Ferrell Center and it's grown so much that we have to have buffet lines. People sit at tables on the court; they sit in the stands. We even set up tables on the concourse the year we won the National Championship. That kind of support is rewarding.

It's also rewarding to hear stories like that of Jack Sanders. He was a diehard Lady Bears fan and he liked to come watch us practice. He became a recognizable face at all our home games. He recently passed away and at his memorial service they played a tape of the National Championship game.

I knew early on during the 2005–06 season that things were going to be different. I had to suspend my starting point guard, Angela Tisdale, for three games. We lost our first game of the season at Missouri and never could figure out a way to beat Oklahoma, which had the sensational freshman Courtney Paris. They beat us twice in the regular season and again in the Big 12 Conference tournament championship game.

As was the case the year before, we played LSU in a regular-season game. It was the first meeting since the Final Four and this time the game was played on their home floor in Baton Rouge.

Before the game, I approached Pokey Chatman, the LSU coach, for the customary handshake. It is usually a pretty harmless ritual, but on this occasion, it proved to be anything but. I remember her saying something to me that shocked me, something I deemed totally unprofessional. There was a television camera nearby and it picked up part of the exchange, focusing on the name "Hightower." Pokey and I had heavily recruited a Texas high schooler named Allison Hightower. She was a McDonald's All-American, the kind of player we never could have gotten a few years earlier. She verbally committed to Baylor but changed her mind and ended up going to LSU. Recruiting can sometimes get a bit nasty

and this was one of those times. I had pretty much forgotten about it.

What I remember Pokey saying that upset me so much
had nothing to do with Allison Hightower. When I went to
shake Pokey's hand my recollection is that she said to
me, "I don't really want to shake your hand, but I am
going to do it for the fans and the TV cameras. I don't like
you and I am sure you don't like me." I was stunned. I
asked if it had to do with Allison Hightower and my recollection is that she said, "Naw, hell no. It's over a lot of
things." I continued across the court to the LSU bench
and shook the hands of the assistants. When I got back to
our bench, I turned to Jennifer Roberts and said, "You
won't believe what she just said to me. I almost went off
on her!"

We lost the game—badly. When I shook Pokey's hand
to congratulate her I said, "What you did before the game
was unprofessional and you need to tell the media what
you said." I told her that if she didn't, I would. No matter
what you feel toward somebody, you don't say it in a pre-
game conversation to another coach.

I never told the media what Pokey said. I told them to
ask her about it. Both Pokey and her athletic director,
Skip Bertman, denied that she said anything unprofessional. I later read that Bertman said I was high strung
and that what happened might have been because we
lost so badly. Nothing was further from the truth.

Regardless of the final score, win or lose, what she did
was unprofessional. We could have won by 20 points or

lost by 50. The score of the ball game had nothing to do with it. It happened before the game. This is a very competitive profession. Some coaches are good buddies. Some coaches don't like each other. I never had a problem with Pokey Chatman until that game. In fact, her mentor, Sue Gunter, was one of the legends of our game and one of the greatest ladies you could ever meet in this profession. Regardless of how Pokey felt about me, prior to a game is not the place to say those things. It's very unfortunate that it got the attention it did, but I still say to this day that it was unprofessional.

Skip Bertman was correct in defending his coach. I respect him for that. What he should not have done was attack me. We have never met and he does not know me. To say that I am high strung, well, I might be intense, passionate, and competitive but never high strung. We must have different interpretations of what that means. And for him to say that I was embarrassed (because it was my most lopsided loss as a head coach)—what an assumption on his part! Was he embarrassed when his team blew a 15-point lead to us in the Final Four? I sure hope not!

After that game, we won nine of the last 10 games and got to the Big 12 championship game, where we lost to Oklahoma. In the NCAA Tournament, we got to the Sweet 16, but lost to Maryland. They went on to win the National Championship.

Once you taste the Sweet 16 and a National Championship, you want to do the same thing year after year. We'll try to do that, but when you are rebuilding and reloading from year to year, it's not always a realistic goal. We want to build a tradition. We want to be able to visit a recruit's home and show them the things that we have accomplished. That's what we're trying to do at Baylor.

Anytime we lose, I think the future looks bleak, but then I wake up the next morning and realize we had a heck of a year. We made it to a third straight Sweet 16. We did it with four freshmen who got valuable playing time. We did it with a sophomore point guard. We had a very good recruiting class. We lost a tremendous senior class, but we've got to keep moving forward because they all graduate sooner or later.

Two weeks after the tournament nearly 1,000 fans gathered at the Ferrell Center for our season-ending appreciation banquet. That was my final public opportunity to thank Sophia Young, who certainly left her mark as perhaps the finest women's player ever to play at Baylor.

She was a two-time Kodak All-America—the first at Baylor to be named twice. She was a person who elevated our program and put us at a level where we were able to win a National Championship. Rightfully, Sophia was named the Most Valuable Player of the 2005 NCAA Tournament.

The 2005–06 season was the hardest year I've ever had because of all that was going on in my personal life. I never went public with the news of my divorce but there was one story that noted that I was no longer wearing my wedding ring. Although never published, my divorce papers eventually became public record.

During the tough times, you see what you're made of. I knew I still had to go out there and be a leader. Regardless of what I was going through, I was there to coach and to lead a team. I could not let my divorce consume me. I had an obligation to the university and the basketball program to do my job. My job was to give that team my undivided attention for two to three hours each day. I think I'm pretty good at remaining focused on the task at hand before I move on to the next one. Basketball was therapeutic for me. It allowed me to get away from all the personal things. That season it allowed me to put one foot in front of the other and keep going. Basketball has and always will provide me with a great sense of relief and a way to move forward in my life.

Epilogue

Fresh Start, Fresh Faces

Before the 2006–07 season even started, I had a feeling it was going to be one of the most challenging I'd experienced in a while. For the first time since I started at Baylor, there was turnover in the coaching staff. Bill Brock, my associate head coach for the past six years, took a similar position at Texas Tech. I replaced him with Karen Aston, who was a top assistant under Jody Conradt when she was at the University of Texas. I also added a fourth assistant, Damion McKinney. He was a high school coach in Dallas with excellent contacts. He was also very active in an AAU program in the Dallas area. I had this fourth opening on my staff for some time, but had never filled it.

Our team was young. Really young. We recruited six freshmen from all parts of the country. There were two from the New York City area including our first ever

McDonald's All-American, a six-foot three-inch center named Danielle Wilson. There were two additional recruits from California, one from Sacramento and one from Chino. But most importantly, there was our new-comer Bernice Mosby, a transfer from Florida.

Bernice was required to sit out the 2005–06 season due to NCAA transfer rules, but she was still able to practice with us every day, often going up against Sophia Young. We had a pretty good idea of how good a player she was and could be. But we still had so many question marks— six freshmen, three sophomores, and only one returning senior, LaToya Wyatt. It would have been Emily Neimann's and Monique Jones' senior years, but they were no longer with the program and we hadn't replaced them. We hoped that Bernice would fill some of the leadership void.

When you are considering a transfer you need to do your homework and a lot of soul-searching. You can't afford to bring in a disruptive player or someone that doesn't fit in. When you first talk to a potential transfer you try to run them off and scare them. You tell them you don't think they can play for you. You tell them you don't think they have what it takes. The bottom line is that players transfer for some reason and, in the end, if they don't work out you can get rid of them

Bernice was up front and forthcoming about why she was dismissed from the Florida team. She had a conflict with her coach, Carolyn Peck. She told me, "I was a prima donna. I thought I was bigger than the program. I was wrong. I am the one responsible. I can't undo what I did but all I'm asking for is a second chance." Bernice had all the right answers to my questions. She said, "I need this in my life." I put a lot of consideration into whether or not I should allow her to transfer. I knew we were losing so many seniors and we needed a more mature, seasoned player. Finally, we decided to approve her transfer.

Bernice certainly lived up to her end of the deal. She ended up being our best player and led us in scoring and rebounding. Looking back, I wish I could have had her for more than just one year. At the time, I didn't know how hard or how long she could play. She was an incredibly talented young woman. There were times, nevertheless, when she couldn't stay on the floor because she couldn't fight through the fatigue. I don't know if it was conditioning or something mental. I wanted her to be able to stay on the floor, especially on the defensive end, but sometimes she just couldn't. I wish we had the time to make her the kind of defensive player we felt she could be. But we only had her for that one year.

Even with Bernice, we still had so much teaching and learning to do. We had an excellent freshman class. Danielle Wilson ended up breaking the school record for blocked shots in a single season. That was a pleasant surprise. With such a large portion of the team comprised of freshmen, it was hard to know what to expect.

When you establish goals they need to be realistic ones. We were starting over. We didn't have the seniors we needed, so we had to keep our expectations real. If we set reasonable goals and exceeded them, the result would be a positive. This was very similar to what we did my first year at Baylor. This time, instead of listing the conference championship as a goal we said, "Finish in the top half of the conference and then maybe we'll get an NCAA bid." These young women knew what to expect in the sense that they were putting on a Baylor uniform and the team had won a National Championship. They knew Baylor was a top 25 program playing in a competitive conference. All they needed was time to get their feet wet and to learn our system.

I tell all my players that their freshman year will be the hardest year of basketball. For many it's their first time away from home. They're out of the comfort zone they had in high school. A perfect example is Whitney Jones, one of my six freshmen. She started one game for us and was averaging 10 minutes a game. Nevertheless, she decided that she was homesick and left school early in the season. She is from West Monroe, Louisiana and ended up enrolling at my alma mater, Louisiana Tech. I told her that she was making a mistake, it was too early for her to leave school, and she shouldn't quit in the middle of the year. If she wanted to transfer, she owed it to herself to complete the full year, but the homesickness won out and she left.

Coaching the team the previous season, while trying to keep my marriage together, was difficult and challenging from a personal perspective. However, the 2006–07 season was my most difficult coaching year. I had to learn the word "patience." I am not by nature a very patient person, but these kids needed to be coached and taught. They made the same mistakes over and over again.

Practices went longer than I liked most days. You had to convince them that they had to work hard on every single play. I was worn out because of all the time I spent on the floor. Coaching such a young team is like a roller coaster ride. One day one of them gets it and the others don't. The next day the others get it and the one that got it the first time doesn't. At some point, I convinced myself that they are all going to get it together. Their heads were spinning, as they began to realize how hard they were going to have to work and practice every day— with only one day off. Eventually, though, they began to understand that they needed to execute the right way every time and, if not, they were going to be held accountable.

We did well that year, with no serious injuries. We kept our goals realistic and exceeded them. We were tied for first place in our conference going into the final weekend of the season. We were picked to finish fourth in the conference, but our players overachieved and we finished third.

The highlight of the season was beating LSU in a game at the Ferrell Center. The atmosphere in the building was electric and there were signs all over the place. Pokey and I were professional. LSU went on to reach the Final Four for the fourth straight year, but just before the tournament began, Pokey announced that she was resigning.

The thing I am most proud of is that of our eight losses, all of them were to ranked teams. In my mind, there were a couple of those losses that we might have won had the ball bounced differently. Overall, we did not have any bad losses. We were in a position where we might have been able to win either of the Texas A&M games but didn't. We lost twice to Oklahoma; they're just better—and bigger—than us right now. I have to give credit where credit is due: Sherri Coale has done a great job coaching there. You have to ask yourself if you're losing to a better team and the answer with Oklahoma was, yes, we were.

I thought we were capable of being a Sweet 16 team until I saw the draw for the NCAA Tournament. We were given a No. 5 seed and, if we were able to beat Tennessee-Chattanooga in the first round, we would then most likely have to play North Carolina State in Raleigh. The game was not being played in their gym, but it was in their town and it was like a home game for them.

We beat Tennessee-Chattanooga, and before the game, our team got to meet my high school coach, Iwana McGee. It was a very emotional meeting because Iwana is battling cancer. I hope the kids picked up something from the experience. I think they did because there weren't many dry eyes in the room. It's all about life's lessons. Here was a woman, battling cancer, who managed to make the trip to Raleigh. She told my mother and Cheryl Gaude that she was going to try and make it because she didn't know if she was going to be around the next year.

That game was also the very emotional and compelling story of Kay Yow, the North Carolina State coach who was also an assistant coach of my 1984 Olympic team. She is an amazing, Christian woman and draws on her unbelievable faith to do what she does. She was suffering from stage-four breast cancer, undergoing chemotherapy, and all the while, still trying to lead her team in the NCAA Tournament.

The intangibles were monumental. I told the kids that there was nothing I could say to them that would compare to what Kay Yow was going through. In addition, she had five seniors in her top seven players and they were playing at home. I thought our team was as focused as it could possibly have been. All you can ask for in a situation like that is to have a chance to win the game and we did. We called the right play. We got the ball to the right person—Bernice. Nevertheless, she ended up too far from the basket when she took the shot. We ended up losing the game in overtime.

Bernice played a terrific game that night under very trying circumstances. She had just learned devastating news: Her family's home in Florida had burned to the ground. Fortunately, no one was injured. She talked to her family back home and they encouraged her to play. I thought it was the right decision, as well. In my opinion, she was the best player on the floor that night. I believe she will have a promising future in the WNBA.

I was happy with the overall way the team performed. However, even after having those freshmen for one year, I still don't know how good they're going be. I'm realistic; it takes time to build a team.

I'm excited about the 2007–08 season. We signed two recruits: Melissa Jones from Colorado and Kelli Griffin from the Houston area. Melissa is a five-foot eleven-inch perimeter player and Kelli is a five-foot eight-inch point guard who missed all of last season with a torn ACL. Kelli, who is from the same high school as Chameka Scott, was ranked as one of the best players in Texas before she got hurt.

We only signed two players because we felt there was going to be a greater need to hold scholarships for players that are going to be seniors in high school next season. We lost two seniors, Bernice Mosby and Latoya Wyatt, so we were down to eight players on scholarship. Melissa and Kelli, make it 10. That means I will now have six available scholarships for 2008–09 because Angela Tisdale will be playing her final season.

That's why it is so important to monitor your scholarships as well as keep an eye on all the talent that is out there. If I signed three or four kids for the season, it would decrease what I could offer the next class.

We also have a new associate head coach, the third in three years. I knew that Karen Aston was going to be a head coach sometime soon and, as it turned out, she accepted the head job at the University of North Carolina-Charlotte. I replaced her with Richard Barron, who was the head women's coach at Princeton. I had gotten to know him over the years and he had always asked if he could use my name as a reference if he was looking for a job. After Karen left, he called again and asked if he could use my name and I said, "Sure, but would you ever consider coming to the Big 12 Conference and being an assistant at Baylor?" And he did.

At the conclusion of every season there are always job openings and rumors that you have to deal with. People are going to speculate and gossip and you have no control over it. You also have no control over someone mentioning your name as a candidate for a particular job. I can't believe some of the stuff that people write. There is absolutely no accountability. In my opinion it's not right or healthy. People hide behind a screen name and write whatever they want to write. I've always said I would make an announcement if my future was going to change. I told the press this past spring, "Have you ever known me not to set up a press conference and say 'this is the way the cow eats cabbage'? And I will."

In a way it's flattering to see my name mentioned for all these openings. This past spring there were some very marquee jobs available: Duke, Louisiana State, Texas, Florida, Michigan, Michigan State, and Arkansas. I have always said that Baylor was good to me and that the university is simply not going to sit there idle while someone tries to steal one of its coaches. I have always felt that Baylor would step up and do the right thing to ensure that I didn't leave. And they did this past spring, signing me to a new contract that pretty much ensures I will be in Waco for the foreseeable future.

I must say that I never anticipated signing the deal on the hood of my car but that is exactly what happened. I was eating chicken nuggets at a local restaurant when the athletic director, Ian McCaw, called me and told me he wanted me to sign the new deal. I had a rather tight schedule and asked him if it could wait until I returned from the WNBA draft. Ian told me he would bring the contract to the restaurant and I could sign it there. The next thing you know, Ian was at my table, contract in hand. I looked it over and said, "I don't know Ian, I haven't had enough time to read it over. I don't know what changes have been made." He assured me that everything was written exactly as we had previously agreed. I said, "OK, I'll sign it. Give me a pen." Then there was a long silence; Ian had forgotten to bring a pen. I told him I had one in my car, so we walked out to the Chick-fil-A parking lot, found a pen, and I signed the new deal on the hood of my car.

Baylor has proven to be such a good fit for me and for my kids. My children really made the decision for me. With all the drama and trauma they had been through with the divorce, whatever they wanted, I was up for it. They wanted to stay. My daughter was a starter as a freshman on both the varsity basketball and softball teams. My son will be in middle school pretty soon. They love it in Waco. Getting the chance to stay at Baylor is what we all wanted. The university gave me that, as well as the opportunity to be me. They appreciate all the hard work we're putting in and the job we're doing. All in all, I think it's a perfect fit.

Afterword

When I look back on the 2007–08 season, I think of it as one of the more remarkable ones in all my years at Baylor. We were in the thick of things for the Big 12 championship, to the point where we would have been regular season champions had we won our final game. We also earned a three seed in the NCAA Tournament. Considering the depleted roster we had, I'm very proud of what we were able to do.

My biggest fear going into the season was that we lacked a go-to player in the post, because Bernice Mosby had graduated. I had always had one before, whether it was Bernice or Sophia Young, but we were now going to have to play and win another way. Bernice had led our team in scoring and rebounding, so she wasn't going to be easy to replace. But even with all the question marks and uncertainties, I was still excited about the season. A lot of roles were going to have to be examined and possibly changed.

Before the season started, we were picked to finish third in the Big 12 Conference, and while that sounded a little optimistic to me, I didn't think it was totally out of line. Replacing Bernice was going to be a big issue. But our underclassmen gained a lot of playing experience the year before and our only senior, Angela Tisdale, was showing signs of becoming a WNBA-caliber player. As a matter of fact, she was later drafted by the Chicago Sky, becoming the sixth player we've had chosen in the WNBA Draft. In fact, in the eight years I've been at Baylor, four of the six players drafted have been first-rounders.

Early on, however, we lost two players who I had hoped would be contributors to our 2007–08 team. A junior college transfer, Kendrea Walker, never even set foot on campus because of academic issues. While she had graduated from junior college, Baylor wouldn't accept a grade from one of her courses. I also had to dismiss one of my players, freshman Latara Darrett. She had played in all 34 games the previous season and even started six of them, but she also continuously broke team rules, and I felt I had no other option but to dismiss her from the team. She's a good kid, not someone that you want to get rid of. Since her dismissal, I have talked to her on several occasions, and she is planning to enroll at Mt. SAC junior college in California.

Our season started out well until we visited Stanford, who beat us pretty badly for our first loss. They had Candice Wiggins—enough said! And they were just a lot more poised than we were. Plus, we had to play them on their home court and they play well there; they even beat Tennessee there not long after they beat us.

But for the next six weeks or so, we really started to become a pretty good basketball team as players accepted roles. We won our next 12 games after the Stanford loss and we were 20–1, tied for first in the Big 12 Conference. Over the course of the season, we beat Oklahoma twice, something we had not been able to do in either of the last two seasons. We never had a go-to player like Candice Wiggins or Candace Parker, but we were pretty balanced offensively. Someone different seemed to step up every game, and it almost had that same feeling as the National Championship season when the kids went out and expected to win every game. We only had one senior, but five of our players were averaging in double figures. We were even ranked as high as No. 5 in the Associated Press Poll at one point.

Then, nine minutes into the game at Kansas State on February 2, Jhasmin Player, one of our captains and top players, went down. And when she didn't get right back up, I knew it was bad because she is a tough kid. She had a torn ACL, which ended her season. We managed to win that game, which was great, and it spoke volumes about the heart of our team. But we never really recovered from Jhasmin's injury. We just didn't have enough depth. I know Geno Auriemma or Pat Summitt can just send in another McDonald's All-American when one of their players goes down, but we don't have that luxury right now. Maybe some day we will.

I sensed this would be a situation from which it would be difficult, if not impossible, to recover, but I never let the players or the fans sense it. In Jhasmin, we lost a player who makes everyone around her better. When she's on the floor and has the ball, the other players only have to catch and finish. With Jhasmin out, we also lost the ability to make transition baskets, which is crucial when you're having trouble with your half-court offense. She's working very hard at rehab, and we expect her to be at full strength for the start of the 2008–09 season.

We sort of hit a wall after our win at Kansas State. We kept working hard in games, but the most difficult part for the staff was trying to figure out a way not to wear the players out in practice. And that was hard, because practice is where you get better. That's where you do your teaching, and that's where competition brings out the best in everyone. We simply didn't have enough bodies to compete. We had to keep them healthy so they could be together on the floor for our games. We did, however, spend more time practicing against the male practice team—the Dream Team.

But what I'll remember for a long time is that the team, as depleted as it was, still went into the final game of the regular season with a chance to win another Big 12 championship. Had we managed to beat either Texas A&M on the road or Oklahoma State at home, we would have been no worse than co-champions. But we couldn't pull it off. As a result, we were the No. 2 seed in the Big 12 Conference Tournament, which was being played in Kansas City.

After receiving a first-round bye, our opening game against Texas in the Big 12 Tournament has to rank as one of the most frustrating and disappointing games in all my years at Baylor. We had beaten Texas at home during the regular season and lost to them in Austin. We played a terrific first half and led by 16 points—but in the end lost the game by 15 points! It was a total meltdown in the second half.

It was such a helpless feeling watching our team. I said at the time that if I hadn't been so young, I might have retired after this one. That's how hard it was. Over the course of the season, we beat some teams that were better than us and we lost a couple of heartbreakers. But this was excruciating to watch. I felt so bad for us. It was like we couldn't lift our arms to even make a basket and everything started to snowball. As a coach, you can only help them in so many ways. You can't make shots.

We still managed to get a No. 3 seed in the NCAA Tournament, and we beat Fresno State in the first round. But just like the year before, we couldn't get past the second round and into the Sweet Sixteen. We lost to an experienced Pittsburgh team that was just a little too strong for us, especially in the post. They had a big senior center named Marcedes Walker, who had been in foul trouble in the first half. But in the second half, she was just too much for us to handle. Had we managed to win that game, we would have had a rematch with Stanford. I've been asked how far I thought the team could go, given the injuries and our depleted roster. I think we did as much as we could with what we had, and many years from now, I am going to look back and realize it was one of our staff's better coaching jobs.

I am anxiously awaiting the 2008–09 season for a number of reasons, not the least of which is the return of my mentor, coach Leon Barmore! My longtime assistant, Jennifer Roberts, had to step away from the game because of health reasons. Because Jennifer had been one of his managers at Louisiana Tech, I called coach Barmore to tell him. Well, one thing led to another, and I finally said to him, "Look. You got out of coaching too young. You've still got a lot to offer, and you sound bored to me. Why don't you come here and help me coach?" I thought he might be ready for a change, because he'd been sitting around doing nothing for years in Ruston.

Coach Barmore still has so much to offer, and this is a way for me to say "thank you" to him for all he's done for women's basketball. He won't have to go to any meetings or stuff like he had to do as a head coach. All he has to do is be an assistant and enjoy the perks. After coming to a couple of our games and seeing the excitement, crowd size, the league we play in, and the fact that when we travel, it's either by bus or by charter plane, it became attractive to him. He just wants to help in any way he can. I think it's going to be great. Also, I am looking forward to working with Rekha Patterson again. She was on my staff as a graduate assistant from 2002–04. I have hired her to be our coordinator of basketball operations.

Coaches Barmore and Patterson aren't the only new faces we're going to have next season. We have a transfer from Arkansas, Whitney Zachariason, who practiced with us last season and will be eligible to play in December. She's a 6' 29 post player who was Miss Basketball in Arkansas as a high school player. We've also signed a transfer from Southern Cal, Morghan Medlock, who will be the second McDonald's All-American to play for me at Baylor. In addition, we will have five freshmen coming into the program. Joining the Lady Bear family will be Brianna Brown (Chandler, Arizona), Terran Condrey (Eufaula, Ala.), Ashley Field (Burnet, Texas), Lindsay Palmer (Tulsa, Oklahoma), and Cherrish Wallace (Pasadena, California).

I expect it to be a very competitive team at a number of positions, even with Angela Tisdale graduating. I am going to miss Angela. She had a tremendous year and was one of the hardest workers I've ever coached. She was also the best shooter I've ever had as a point guard at Baylor.

We'll have three seniors on the team in 2008–09, including Jhasmin Player. The others are forwards Rachel Allison and Jessica Morrow. Rachel was our second leading scorer in 2007–08 and Jessica was our fourth. Also, junior Danielle Wilson and sophomores Kelli Griffin and Melissa Jones will be returning too.

I'm looking forward to this coming season because, for the first time, we are taking a foreign tour in August to Vancouver, Canada, where we will play two Canadian teams in exhibitions. With such a young team and so many new faces, that is going to be a big help. We also will play in the Virgin Islands around Thanksgiving and will have a rematch with Stanford, in Waco, as well.

223

As for me, I still spend my time coaching and going to my kids' games. My son, Kramer, a seventh grader, continues to play football, basketball, and baseball, and it's hard to believe it won't be long before he's in high school. My daughter, Makenzie, is driving now, and she will be a junior in the fall of 2008. An outstanding student as well as athlete, she is already receiving questionnaires from colleges about her basketball skills and academic record, but she isn't going anywhere. She wants to play for me, and I want her to play for me. I just hope it works out.

Acknowledgments

These enterprises never happen in a vacuum. My name may be on the cover, but it is there only thanks to the tireless work of many others.

My support staff has remained pretty much intact since I came to Baylor. Julie Bennett is our media relations director. She helps me walk that fine line between what is office business only—and what the media would like to consider everyone's business. Our athletic trainer is Alex Olson and I have grown very comfortable with his knowledge and how he takes great care of our players. I know if someone cannot play, it is not because Alex hasn't pursued every avenue to get that player game ready. Shaun McPherson joined us my second year, as our strength and conditioning coach. I can depend on him to keep the players in the best condition possible. Every time I hear a player complain that Shaun is overworking them, I know he is doing exactly what needs to be done to keep the players strong and well-conditioned for play. Rick May and Lori Fogleman, our radio announcers, bring our game to life for the fans that can't be in attendance. They have been with me from the start and are avid Lady Bear fans.

Debbie Penney is our administrative assistant and she has been involved with the program since I first came to Baylor. Debbie is the most important person in my office. She helps me more than I could ever explain and she has spent countless hours helping me with this book. It is a great positive to have a support group where there is a comfort level in that everyone knows each other well and everyone is focused on what is best for the women's basketball program.

I especially want to acknowledge all of the players I have coached, as well as the managers, the student-trainers, and the graduate assistants who have been part of this program—your contributions are invaluable.

—KM

I would first like to thank Kim Mulkey for agreeing to do this project. She was at all times available and accommodating and I know she secretly wants to be an English teacher in her next life. My agent, Colleen Mohyde of the Doe Coover Agency, helped get the process started and remained an unflagging booster throughout. Frances Kennedy, also at Doe Coover, was a big help. My editor at Da Capo Press, Kevin Hanover, was a model of patience and understanding during the whole process, no small feat given the inherent procrastination tendencies of the author. He believed in this project from the outset and shepherded it through.

I also could not have done this project without the help of the key people in Kim's life. In Ruston, Louisiana, Leon Barmore generously donated his time and thoughts and even bought lunch at the Blue Light. The Tutens, Mary Belle and Allen, were kind enough to drive me around Ruston and share their stories about Kim. So, too, was the man who started the Lady Techster basketball program, F. Jay Taylor. Although we never did connect in person, Buddy Davis of the *Ruston Daily Leader* was always ready to help with stories about Kim and the Lady Techsters.

In Hammond, Louisiana, I owe a lot of gas money to Dru Mulkey, who was my personal chauffeur for three days and who shared with me her memories of her daughter, her family, and the area.

—PM

Made in the USA
Las Vegas, NV
17 April 2023

70718435R00152